Dare to Dream: learning journeys of Bangladeshi, Pakistani and Somali women

By Jane Ward and Rachel Spacey

promoting adult learning

European Union
European Social Fund
Investing in jobs and skills

©2008 National Institute of Adult Continuing Education
(England and Wales)
21 De Montfort Street
Leicester
LE1 7GE

Company registration no. 2603322
Charity registration no. 1002775

NIACE has a broad remit to promote lifelong learning opportunities for adults. NIACE works to develop increased participation in education and training, particularly for those who do not have easy access because of class, gender, age, race, language and culture, learning difficulties or disabilities, or insufficient financial resources.

You can find NIACE online at www.niace.org.uk

European Union
European Social Fund
Investing in jobs and skills

The European Social Fund is a European Union initiative that supports activities to extend employment opportunities and develop a skilled workforce.

Cataloguing in Publication Data
A CIP record of this title is available from the British Library
Designed and typeset by Book Production Services, London
Printed and bound in the UK by Latimer Trend

ISBN: 978 1 86201 375 9

Contents

Acknowledgements

This publication owes a great deal to the hard work and enthusiasm shown by the researchers who interviewed Bangladeshi, Pakistani, and Somali women in their communities. They were also involved in the identification of emerging themes and in commenting on the draft: Aleya Chowdhury, Yasmin Chowdhury, Ruqia Farah, Noorjahan Logde, Samina Mahmoud, Jeba Maleque, Jorna Monshur, Idil Abdi Osman, and Sudha Vemuri.

The authors would also like to thank all the women who kindly gave their time to be interviewed and shared their stories. We thank the staff who arranged visits to their learning organisation, those who completed the online questionnaire and those who were interviewed by telephone for their contributions. Thanks also to the organisations who hosted research visits:

Preston College
Liverpool Community College
Manchester Adult Education Service
Shama Women's Centre, Leicester
Tower Hamlets College

We would also like to thank NIACE colleagues who have contributed to this project in a variety of ways: Neil Goodall, Marie Kerwin, Jan Novitzky,

Anne O'Grady, Judith Gawn, Chris Taylor, Phil Hughes, Jan Eldred, Peter Lavender and the Research Team

We are grateful for the support of the European Social Fund in funding this work. Adult Learners' Week/Sign Up Now is part-funded by the European Social Fund. Visit www.esf.gov.uk'. This research report contributes by investigating barriers and enablers for Bangladeshi, Pakistani and Somali women to access learning.

Foreword

It is clear from this powerful report that all of the Bangladeshi, Pakistani and Somali women interviewed believed, in the words of one of them, that learning English is 'the key of life', and in the words of another 'learning is better than not learning. However, well over sixty percent of the women interviewed are not currently engaged in learning.

NIACE undertook the research with the support of the European Social Fund to identify barriers to learning experienced by women from the three communities where women's participation is dramatically lower than for the population at large. In a companion volume, (*Are We Closing the Gap: A NIACE briefing on participation in learning by adults from ethnic minority groups*, Aldridge *et al* 2008) NIACE analysed results from the English Local Labour Force survey to identify the scale of under-representation.

Its key findings present challenges to the communities in which the interviewees live, for providers and government alike – '*Dare to dream*' articulates a gap between women's aspirations and the opportunities open to them. Some of the barriers lie in the lack of value afforded to women's learning in some families and wider communities; and wider discrimination against women in institutions and wider society.

Its challenge to public policy makers is to design programmes to overcome barriers and to release the energies, abilities and enthusiasm of people for whom current provision does not work. Addressing that challenge is of key importance in securing community cohesion and a society where everyone can fulfil their dreams.

Dare to Dream recognises that the position of women from the same groups can differ dramatically. It maps a journey of changing values and widening provision as well as pockets of persistent exclusion.

I am grateful to my colleagues Jane Ward and Rachel Spacey for leading the work, to the group of community researchers who conducted the interviews, to the women who agreed to be interviewed, to the providers who contributed and to the European Social Fund for the financial support it provided for the work to be undertaken.

Brecht observed that we should measure our civilisation by the way it treated those who benefited least from it. *Dare to Dream* suggests we have a long way to go to make lifelong learning accessible to all Britain's communities and in particular to all Britain's women.

Alan Tuckett

Director, NIACE

Executive Summary

This research set out to investigate the learning journeys of Bangladeshi, Pakistani and Somali women,[1] with a particular emphasis on hindrances to participation in learning and the actions which enhance learning for the most disadvantaged women within these groups. We focus on these women because research consistently shows that Bangladeshi, Pakistani and Somali have fewer English language skills, are less likely to secure sustainable employment, have lower incomes and have fewer opportunities to participate in social and civic society than women from other ethnic groups (Atubo and Batterbury 2001, Aston et al 2007, Botcherby 2006, Tackey *et al.* 2006). The cumulative effect is that some women from these groups are amongst are the most disadvantaged women in the UK.

The research complements the quantitative findings of a recent NIACE report into participation in learning amongst adults from minority ethnic communities (Aldridge *et al.* 2008). This work provides a stark illustration of the exclusion of Bangladeshi, Pakistani and Somali women from learning. It identifies a huge gap between the current overall rates of participation in learning, (71 per cent of white adults of working age) and Bangladeshi (34 per cent) and Pakistani women (42 per cent). The study also finds that many Somali women share this pattern of exclusion from learning. These findings pose what the study describes as an 'extreme challenge' for those concerned with inclusion and equality. This study aims to contribute to addressing this huge challenge by investigating the hindrances to learning and approaches that work.

We interviewed 100 Bangladeshi, Pakistani and Somali women from different backgrounds between January and March 2008; 62 who are not currently taking part in organised learning and 38 who are learning Engish . Bilingual community researchers identified and interviewed the 62 women who are not presently engaged in organised education in order to develop our understanding of the different circumstances and perspectives that influence their participation. We then focused on the learning journeys of women with few skills in English language because lack of English is a major factor in societal exclusion. We also interviewed 38 women who are currently learning English to hear what, for them, made the difference to accessing English language provision, staying the course and moving on. We also investigated provider perspectives through five case study visits, ten telephone interviews with tutors and a web survey, which drew eleven responses.

Our findings provide an emphatic illustration of the differential experiences and factors affecting participation in learning of women in these groups. The conclusion we draw from this is that different strategies are required to ensure that all, especially the most oppressed and marginalised, are reached.

---

1. The terms Pakistani, Bangladeshi and Somali we have adopted are the terms the women involved in our research used to describe their ethnic origin. However they also made us aware that notions of identity are complex and they can have multiple identities, for example some of the Somali women who came to Britain from another European country would also describe themselves as European.

Significant findings

1. The research illustrates that Bangladeshi, Pakistani and Somali women are extremely heterogeneous. There is diversity within these ethnic groups as well as differences and common experiences that cut across them, and the evidence illuminates some of the vast differences in their circumstances. Factors such as educational backgrounds, marital status, age, life stage, personal and family attitudes and experiences all have the potential to make a difference to access to, and chances of succeeding in, learning.

2. The women we studied faced different types of obstacles to learning, and combinations of these barriers resulted in differential levels of access to learning. These broadly accord with *Cross's* model (1981) that categorises barriers to student engagement as ***situational, dispositional and institutional***, and the factors McGivney (2001) identifies as limiting access to learning; personal, cultural, practical, psychological and institutional.

    *   **personal and cultural** – the women's own, husband's, family's and community attitudes and expectations of women's place and role

    *   **practical** – gender oppression – restrictions and violence from families, especially husbands, poor health, old age, caring responsibilities, lack of time

    *   **psychological** – lack of confidence, feeling too old or too sick to learn

    *   **Institutional** – lack of information and advice, classes not at the right level, located in inaccessible locations at unsuitable times, fees, lack of affordable childcare.

    The findings demonstrate why the women we studied are not participating in learning. We know that many women face the same barriers, especially those related to childcare responsibilities. Why are the rates of participation in learning for Pakistani, Bangladeshi and Somali women significantly and consistently lower than those of other groups if they face similar barriers?

    Answers might lie in the nature, intensity and interactions of different hindrances to learning in the lives of Pakistani, Bangladeshi and Somali women. They are more likely to get married than women from other groups and marriage is associated with lower participation. They are more likely to have larger families and less likely to use child carers which means they can be unable to access learning for longer periods of their life. Confidence is frequently cited as a barrier to learning for women from all groups. It becomes a major deterrent when combined with other factors, in particular lack of English.

    Our study reveals the ways in which this limits autonomy and freedom to go out independently which hinders ability to travel to classes. Low levels of English also restrict opportunities to access other vocational, personal or community learning. Different permutations of the above factors combined with the additonal layers of language barriers, cultural expectations and in some cases opposition to learning could account for the lower overall participation rates of Bangladeshi, Pakistani and Somali women. A comparative study could surface further explanations.

3. Attitudinal factors are a powerful determinant of women's learning. As in any community, these attitudes are diverse. The primary attitudes restricting access to learning relate to expectations of women's roles. Over time, views have started to shift and have become more liberal so that some, but not all, women now have fewer restrictions placed on their lives, especially the young women growing up in the UK.

4. The majority of women interviewed are married or expect to get married and this has a bearing on their own views and aspirations as well as the attitudes of others, especially as research indicates a correlation between marriage and lower rates of participation in learning. For most, marriage and becoming a mother is an important goal, although younger women are more likely to study further or work between leaving school and marriage. Domestic duties are still regarded as the primary responsibility of women. Some women are free to make their own decisions about taking up learning, most need the approval of their husbands and families but said they are 'allowed' to learn if their duties do not 'suffer', and a small but significant minority are forbidden from accessing learning outside the home.

5. Life stage and age are powerful determinants of women's access to learning. Unmarried young women tend to have more freedom to study or work. The dominant trend is to stop either on marriage or when they have their first baby. Some never return to learning whilst others next think about learning English when their children start school or even wait until they leave home. By then they have lost time. This reinforces their disadvantage and women who took this decision now find learning harder. Looking back, they often regret not having completed their studies.

6. Caring for children is the major practical barrier to taking up organised learning. The women, like all mothers, face the choice of whether to stay home with their children or to leave them to go out to study or work. Many make positive choices not to leave their babies and young children in the care of others. They want to spend this period with their children and believe this will give them the best start in life. As it is not uncommon to have families of five or more children this means they do not access learning for a longer period. Those who do want to learn, like the rest of the population, find that time and lack of family support and affordable childcare hinders access. The number of affordable childcare places offered by learning organisations is limited so not available to all.

7. Other practical barriers are caring responsibilites for elders or sick family members that usually take precedence over learning. Provision far from home is a barrier for women who are not able to travel independently, as is the need to juggle classes with other responsibilities such as collecting children from school. Potential costs deter some women and lack of information means that others never discover a class. Some respondents reported a scarcity of women only provision that excludes women not allowed to learn in mixed environments.

8. Some women not in learning describe themselves as too old to learn. They feel they have missed their time to learn, have no need, are no longer capable, or it is not appropriate for older women to learn. In contrast, women aged over 60 who are learning are very positive about it although they tend to regret waiting. Poor health is another factor preventing access to learning. This is often related to age although not exclusively so.

9. Gender oppression is a major barrier to learning. A small minority of families hold rigid views that a married women's sole role is related to household duties: domestic labour and caring for her husband, children, other family members and the home. The women in these circumstances are marginalised, struggle to gain any degree of power and autonomy over their lives and are not allowed to access organised learning.

10. Evidence from women learners, learning organisers and teachers offered a powerful testimony to the importance and effectiveness of community outreach approaches. Many of the strategies adopted are not new but are those developed and practised since the 1970s. However, in many places witout outreach they have fallen out of use as demand for ESOL from groups such as migrant workers has filled classes (Ward 2007). McGivney (2001) observes that the concept of outreach work is rediscovered by different generations of education policy makers and practitoners on a regular basis and stresses the need to reflect on and learn from established practice to inform their developments. The community outreach work described by respondents in this study provides one source for this reflection.

Community outreach strategies based on word of mouth emerged as the most successful strategy for reaching the women and attracting them into learning. Within this, different approaches are appropriate for women in different situations. Failure to recognise and respond to this can mean that the most marginalised women remain outside organised learning provision. Specific and effective approaches put forward by providers and learners to reach the women furthest from learning include home visits, befriending schemes, work with families and home tuition.

11. Other effective approaches are offering appropriate provision in easily accessible spaces regarded as safe or trustworthy by the community. Using creative social activities and interesting and enjoyable taster sessions and events to attract and enthuse women was effective. These must be followed with provision offered on terms which enable the women to take it up. Childcare is essential. Location, cost, women only spaces, flexibility, interesting, relevant content and teachers with awareness, understanding and experience of working in communities are other important ingredients.

12. Addressing the challenges of supporting women to achieve is critical. Learners articulated this in relation to a combination of what they referred to as 'good teaching' and support. Good teaching means a teacher they can understand and who understands them, interesting and challenging learning content, praise and recognition of achievement. Teachers cited established quality measures such as initial and formative assessment, tutorials, and Individual Learning Plans. These are of course common to all learning, but the research highlights the importance of ensuring learning and support is tailored to the particular needs and interests of these women.

13. One of the strongest messages is that for many of these women, structured learning must be complemented by strong learner-teacher relationships, support from other learners, mentoring and buddying schemes, role models and social activity which glues them into learning and inspires and enables them to progress. Social activities are used by teachers to broaden knowledge and provide opportunities for using and practising English. The women of all ages find in them a valuable means of fostering friendships and supportive relationships. They encourage each other to learn and for women who are facing home or community disapproval, they break down isolation and engender a sense of solidarity and support that helps them to continue.

14. Once in learning, the women usually become motivated to continue. Although women have their own dreams for their futures, providers can be influential. The women we interviewed frequently set their sights low, choosing gendered occupations such as cleaning, factory machining, working with children, health and social care and beauty. Reasons for this include acceptability, and the constraints of English. However, while lower paid or lower status employment might be realistic options for some women, the horizons of others appear to be limited in part by a lack of suitable information, advice, and guidance and progression

pathways to higher-level courses and occupations. Women who attend provision that offers vocational information and advice and encouragement supported by bridges to progress tend to aim higher than others.

15. The research revealed interesting perspectives on the notion of community. The majority of women interviewed choose to live in areas where there are high numbers of people with a similar background. This is usually a positive choice made for reasons common to most people; the desire to live near friends and family with strong social and support networks and amenities in easy reach and to feel safe. Where the women avoid their English neighbours it is usually for reasons of safety as they experience real or actual threats of crime and harassment and some are subjected to racism.

There are relatively high levels of involvement in communal leisure activities, informal support networks, or voluntary organisations in their own ethnic groups. In contrast there is a noticeable lack of activity outside, and only a small minority of women volunteer or intend to volunteer in the future. Women engaged in learning reported more use of amenities but in general not greater involvement in mixed community activity. English is one of a number of reasons for this, but lack of interest or inclination, lack of time or opportunity or no information or encouragement from community organisations were also cited.

This suggests that English language skills might be a condition for involvement, but by themselves will not automatically bring about greater community cohesion. Learning can provide some of the conditions for fostering relationships between different groups. However, we found little evidence of learning that had the specific aim of fostering cohesion either in discrete groups or in mixed community based groups and more models for this are urgently needed.

Planning and outreach framework

We have drawn on our findings to develop the framework below that can be used to support the identification of need in an area and planning of focused strategies to formulate an inclusive response. This framework identifies four different types of women who have different learning aspirations and/or face different barriers to learning. The inner squares indicate strategies for attracting and supporting these different groups into learning. The lines between the groups are dotted to illustrate that the boundaries between the groups are porous. In other words some women may have attributes from adjacent groups and others move between the groups at different stages. Similarly outreach strategies are not necessarily restricted to any one type and different approaches might be effective at different stages.

Planning and outreach framework

Learning positive

Positive attitudes + few/no practical barriers

Appropriate signposting
Appropriate IAG
Interesting provision
Progression routes

Learning optimistic

Positive attitudes + some practical and/or physical barriers

Outreach workers/learning ambassadors
Childcare/crèche provision
Local classes
Flexible provision
Allow to leave and return
Support during maternity leave
Flexible timing
Women only provision
Taster activities
Relevant content
Appropriate IAG
Appropriate progression routes

Childcare commitments
Caring responsibilities
Lack of time
Distance to provision

Childcare commitments (might plan to learn at a later stage)
Caring responsibilities
Poor health
Age

Promotion using role models
Persuaders
Social activities
Home tuition/street groups

+
leanring optimistic strategies

Befrienders
Family mediators
Home tuition

+
learning optimistic strategies

Gender oppression
Domestic violence

Negative attitudes + some physical and practical Barriers

Learning Negative

Positive attitudes + severe gender oppression, practical and physical barriers

Learning pessimistic

Learning positive women are highly motivated to learn and face minimal serious restrictions or hindrances to learning. For these women the challenge is one of supply; to direct resources to offer enough learning to satisfy this appetite. However, this alone will be insufficient. Those offering learning will need to ensure they do everything possible to enable women to stay with it, to make progress in learning, to raise their aspirations and set them on the path to achieving these aspirations.

Learning optimistic women would like to learn but face practical and/or physical obstacles such as lack of good quality affordable childcare, accessible, relevant provision, or lack of time. Their options are limited by practical barriers that must be considered when planning learning and recruiting women. Bridges to help make entry not only possible but easy are needed. Once engaged, women will need ongoing support to assist them to stay and progress.

Learning negative women are not currently interested in learning. They face barriers such as domestic or caring responsibilities or very poor health. Some can manage or get by and are not motivated to progress further. Others have made a decision not to learn at this stage but might be persuaded now or in the future. Others are resistant for health reasons or because they consider themselves too old to learn.

Learning pessimistic women would like to learn but are unable to access learning outside the home because they are fettered by gender oppression, domestic burdens or ill health. They are unlikely to be able to access learning outside the home as they live in circumstances in which they have few choices or are denied opportunities for autonomous decision-making.

Only the learning negative group is resistant to learning. Women in the other groups would like to learn but face different hindrances to learning. Recognising the differences in women's freedom to choose, and the different nature of the constraints on their choices highlights the complexity of this divergence. It follows, therefore, that different strategies and solutions are needed to reach different women. The signposting that can get some to class will go nowhere to touch the lives of women tied to the home. Reaching those who are most isolated and oppressed poses greater challenges. The strategies most appropriate for each group are outlined in the inner squares

Teachers, outreach workers and champions must be equipped with the skills and understanding to work in this manner and with each other as well as the myriad individuals, front line workers and agencies that also have a stake in these neighbourhoods. These approaches must draw on knowledge and experience accumulated from the past, they might also demand new ways of thinking and working, and they will almost certainly pose challenges. However, they must be tackled in pursuit of a more equal and just society in which the most excluded Bangladeshi, Pakistani and Somali women are empowered to move from the margins and gain more independence and equality.

1. Introduction

Bangladeshi, Pakistani and Somali women[2] are amongst the most disadvantaged adults in British society and they have the lowest levels of participation and achievement in organised learning. This research investigates their learning journeys. It examines factors that obstruct their participation in organised learning and explores ways in which these obstacles can best be overcome.

Pakistani, Bangladeshi and Somali women have fewer English language skills, (Tackey *et al.* 2006) are less likely to secure sustainable employment and have fewer opportunities to participate in social and civic society than women from other groups, indicating that they are amongst are the most excluded women in the UK. At the same time they are highlighted in a number of policy initiatives, notably those concerned with community cohesion, citizenship and employment. Learning in general, and English language proficiency in particular, could help liberate these women to take more control over their lives, gain more independence and autonomy and enhance their social and economic position. This study undertakes an in-depth qualitative examination of the factors that affect participation in learning for the women from these groups who are least likely to take part in organised education that could offer them access routes to greater equality and social justice.

The research complements the quantitative findings of a recent NIACE report into participation in learning amongst adults from minority ethnic communities (Aldridge *et al.* 2008). This work provides a stark illustration of the exclusion of Bangladeshi, Pakistani and Somali women from learning. It identifies a huge gap between the current participation in learning of white adults of working age (71 per cent) and Bangladeshi (34 per cent) and Pakistani women (42 per cent) and finds that many Somali women share this pattern of exclusion from learning. These findings pose what the study describes as an 'extreme challenge' for those concerned with inclusion and equality.

Under representation in learning is only one of a number of disadvantages that add up to the persistence of gender and race based inequalities for women from these groups. Societal inequities are the context for the more personal and community factors that emerge in the research. The following examples are significant in that they demonstrate the multi faceted nature of inequalities, which are deeper seated for many Bangladeshi, Pakistani and Somali women. We suggest, that although learning alone cannot overcome inequalities, women in general, and from these groups in particular are more likely to advance in society when supported by the critical understanding, knowledge and skills that learning can offer.

---

2. The terms Pakistani, Bangladeshi and Somali we have adopted are the terms the women involved in our research used to describe their ethnic origin. However they also made us aware that notions of identity are complex and they can have multiple identities, for example some of the Somali women who came to Britain from another European country would also describe themselves as European.

Society has changed in many ways since the 1970s when the Equal Pay Act 1970 outlawed discrimination in pay between men and women and the Sex Discrimination Act 1975 and the Race Relations Act 1976 made discrimination on the grounds of gender and race, colour, nationality, or ethnic or national origin unlawful. Yet the battle for equality is far from won. The life chances of some women have undoubtedly been transformed, but we do not have to dig very deep to find that in terms of race and class many women's lives have changed little[3]. Discrimination is still ubiquitous and new forms, such as Islamophobia, have emerged.

Economic and political powers remain male dominated. By and large, women are no longer expected to spend their whole lives at home looking after men and children, but in general women still bear the burden of domestic work and childcare and earn less than men[4]. They now have rights to paid maternity leave and there are more nursery places[5] but every year thousands of pregnant workers are treated unfairly at work[6]. Respondents told us about pregnant women being refused access to English classes because they will damage retention and achievement figures. The gap between women and men's pay has narrowed but is still around 12 per cent and is lower for Pakistani, Bangladeshi and Somali women.[7] In public life there are now more women in parliament, but still only 126 women MPs compared to 518 men, only 5 women in the cabinet and no female Bangladeshi, Pakistani or Somali MPs[8].

Many sections of society now appreciate cultural diversity and recognise the contributions of people from black and ethnic minorities to communities, workplaces, sports, and culture[9]. Even so, minority ethnic women in general fare worse than white women, and among them Bangladeshi, Pakistani and Somali women are the most excluded. Overt discrimination in public services and education has diminished, but unequal access and differential achievement persists. Research suggests that factors such as teacher expectations and possible job opportunities may have much to do with success or failure[10]. Bangladeshi, Pakistani and Somali women are least represented amongst high achievers; for example they are least likely to gain a degree or equivalent, become an MP or local councillor, sit as a judge, be a director of a FTSE100 company or chair an NHS board. They are most likely to be outside the labour market looking after their home and family. Although there are differences within groups, the highest overall rates of income poverty in the UK are found in the Bangladeshi (65 per cent), Pakistani (55 per cent) and Black African (45 per cent) groups and the lowest in the White British (20 per cent) group (Platt 2007). Bangladeshi, Pakistani, and African women have the highest rates of unemployment, and those who do work are, in general, paid less on average than white women and men. They have the poorest health and live in poor housing[11].They count amongst the one in four women estimated to be affected by domestic violence in their lifetime, are subjected to forced marriages, and every year women are murdered by families in so called 'honour killings'[12].

---

3. See http://www.whywomen.org.uk/Downloads/Statistics.doc (accessed June 2 2008)

4. http://83.137.212.42/sitearchive/eoc/Default1233.html?page=20519 (accessed June 2 2008)
5. http://www.equalities.gov.uk/about/government_women.htm (accessed June 2 2008)
6. http://83.137.212.42/sitearchive/eoc/Default1233.html?page=20519 (accessed June 2 2008)
7. http://www.equalities.gov.uk/about/government_women.htm (accessed Jun 2 2008)
8. http://www.equalities.gov.uk/public_life/key_facts.htm (accessed June 2 2008)
9. http://www.irr.org.uk/2002/november/ak000003.html (accessed June 2 2008)
10. ibid
11. http://www.equalities.gov.uk/publications/EthnicMinorityWomen.pdf (accessed June 2 2008)
12. http://www.independent.co.uk/news/uk/home-news/a-question-of-honour-police-say-17000-women-are-victims-every-year-780522.html (accessed June 2 2008)

Racism still features in many of their lives. It is not surprising, therefore, that four in ten Asian women say they are 'very worried' about racist attacks[13]. The far right British National Party is active and gaining support. Refugees and asylum seekers are vilified in some sections of the press and these attitudes spill over into sections of the wider population. Islamophobia has emerged since 9/11 and the London bombings. This form of racism is expressed through harassment and violence against Muslims, with Muslim women wearing veils as one of the targets. A recent study by the Joseph Rowntree Trust (JRF 2008) revealed telling examples of faith based prejudice against Muslims, concluding that it is not always clear whether the discrimination they encounter is on the grounds of race or faith.

The causes of Bangladeshi, Pakistani and Somali women's differential achievement are rooted in deep-seated social, political and economic structures and patriarchal power that perpetuate inequalities. Consequently, many of the solutions lie in challenge and change across different arenas and institutions. However, the reluctance of those holding power and privilege to forego it should not be underestimated. Set against this is the fact that people have agency. They don't have to wait for change to be given to them but can engage in individual and collective action and struggle for equality in personal, political and economic spheres.

Adult learning is a powerful weapon in this struggle, providing a route out of disadvantage as well as the skills and knowledge needed for fighting oppression and discrimination. We acknowledge that it is only one factor rather than a sole solution, but research suggests that alongside other interventions it can make a positive difference to women's lives. English language is particularly important to enable women to inform themselves, improve their economic circumstances and employment opportunities, develop confidence, speak out, raise their aspirations and follow their life choices.

A thorough analysis of the bigger picture of societal discrimination and inequalities is beyond the scope of this work. It is, however, the backdrop for our exploration of the ways in which access to learning can support women to take more control over their lives and an illustration of the reasons this is important. We recognise that some Pakistani, Bangladeshi and Somali women do reach higher education, attain higher-level qualifications, secure well-paid employment and are successful in civil society. Our emphasis is on the women in these groups who are furthest from these achievements. English language, as one of the contributors to this exclusion, is a particular focus.

Section 3 provides a brief overview of the context for this study with reference to some of the key policy agendas. It also draws out some important findings from the research literature in relation to the learning and employment experiences of Bangladeshi, Pakistani and Somali women.

Sections 4 and 5 present the findings of the research. In Section 4 we explore the experiences of the women we interviewed. There is a more in- depth focus on the lives of the women not involved in formal or informal learning in this section although we have included views and experiences of the learning women where they offer alternative perspectives. We consider the women's educational background and experiences, their own and the attitudes of their families and communities towards women's education, their views on learning English and their hopes and dreams for the future.

---

13. http://www.wrc.org.uk/downloads/WRC%20Why%20Women%20Report.pdf (accessed June 2 2008)

In Section 5 we present the views of women currently engaged in organised learning, to explore what helps women to gain access and succeed. We interweave the stories of their learning journeys with the views of learning providers who have successfully engaged with women from Bangladeshi, Pakistani and Somali communities to reveal what can be done to make a difference.

Finally, in Section 6 we come to some conclusions and suggest a framework to support providers and those planning learning to identify the various barriers to accessing learning faced by different women and develop differentiated engagement strategies to address them. We then make recommendations for policy and practice.

2. Methods

This research set out to explore the learning journeys of Bangladeshi, Pakistani and Somali women. Our research questions were: 'What are the attitudes to learning of Bangladeshi, Pakistani and Somali women' and 'What impedes their learning journeys and what enables them to access and progress in learning?' We adopt a feminist perspective which for us means framing the research within a conceptual focus on the gender inequalities and patriarchal power and control that affect women's lives.

Data collection

We gathered data between January and March 2008. We undertook a literature review to identify the latest research information on participation in learning by Bangladeshi, Pakistani and Somali women. We found there was little research into the learning, in particular English language learning, of the most marginalised women from these groups. The review enabled us to identify both recurring themes and gaps in the research knowledge that informed the formulation of questions for our study.

We interviewed 100 women; 62 women who are not taking part in organised learning and 38 who attend English language classes. We talked to the 62 Bangladeshi, Pakistani and Somali women from a range of backgrounds who are not presently engaged in organised education in order to develop our understanding of the different circumstances and perspectives that might influence their participation. We asked about their lives, their dreams and aspirations, their views on learning, what stops them participating in organised learning and what would help them to start.

We employed bilingual community researchers to identify interviewees and conduct the interviews. This was to ensure that we reached a broad sample of women. The interviewers were trusted so the women were more relaxed and open in their interviews, and language barriers did not inhibit the conversations. We are aware, however, that this means the particular perspectives and views of the researchers could also be reflected in the research as these could colour the way in which they posed their questions and probed the women's responses.

We then focused on the learning journeys of women with few skills in English language as these are the most under represented group of learners, and lack of English is a major factor in their societal exclusion. To inquire into successful strategies for supporting women to participate in education we interviewed, in group interviews, 38 women who are currently learning English to hear what, for them, made the difference to accessing learning, staying the course and moving on.

Finally we investigated provider perspectives on overcoming barriers to participation and effectively engaging Bangladeshi, Pakistani and Somali women through five case study visits, ten telephone interviews with tutors and a web survey which elicited eleven full responses. The interviews and visits were undertaken with Further Education colleges, Adult and Community learning and voluntary and community sectors providers in different parts of England to provide a sectoral and geographical spread.

Data analysis

As we analysed the data, the community researchers worked with us to provide their insights into the data and themes emerging from the interviews. They also commented on a draft of the publication. This added a rich extra layer of analysis informed by the cultural contexts of the participants. We have used the women's own words to illustrate the findings set out in the text. Many chose to be quoted in their own name and others chose a pseudonym.

3. Context

As stated in the introduction, the recent NIACE briefing on participation in learning by adults from minority ethnic groups (Aldridge *et al.* 2008) highlights the comparatively low levels of participation in learning of Bangladeshi, Pakistani and Somali women. This section draws together the findings from this study and other relevant published research and policy documents to outline the context in which our research is located. We examine this in the following sections:

● Educational experience

● Employment

● Participation in learning

● English language

● Community participation.

One of the problems besetting research in this area, as recognised by the Office for National Statistics (ONS 2007) is that it is almost impossible to source reliable, up-to-date demographic data on immigrants and their language learning needs. In their study of migration and gender, Kofman *et al.* (2005) conclude that gender and migration are under-researched, and family related migration, the migration pattern of the Pakistani and Bangladeshi women in this study in particular, has received very little attention. We have drawn on available data, including the Labour Force Survey which, despite some limitations, does indicate trends.

There are 352,568 Pakistani and 139,075 Bangladeshi women in England and Wales according to the 2001 census[14]. The overall Somali population in the UK was recorded as 43,473. Since the date of the census more Somalis have arrived to seek asylum in the UK and an unknown number of Somali refugees have migrated here as secondary migrants from other European countries. A more recent briefing sheet (ICAR 2007) suggests that the number of women of Somali origin is more likely to be in the region of 90,000. One of the factors hampering research is that statistical data, on the whole, subsumes data relating to Somalis within more general African categories (Aldridge *et al.* 2007).

Recent research addressing the participation in education of Pakistani and Bangladeshi women in Britain is very limited, although the research in relation to employment for Bangladeshi, Pakistani and Somali women is more abundant. As the issues affecting learning and employment can be similar and inter-related, we identify relevant themes from recent literature that considers the employment of Pakistani and Bangladeshi women, including Aston *et al.* (2007), Botcherby (2006) and Tackey *et al.* (2006). There are relatively few qualitative studies addressing the situation of Somali women in general and almost no studies of Somali women and learning. We have drawn on wider studies to illuminate issues for Somali women's participation in education.

---

14. Figures taken from Table S102 – sex and country of birth by ethnic group from the Office for National Statistics – national report for England and Wales.

Educational experience

Educational experience is important, as many studies, for instance Aldridge *et al.* (2008) have demonstrated that this affects access to adult learning. It must be stressed that it is difficult to make assertions about whole groups since experiences of schooling can differ greatly. We see this in the educational backgrounds of women who came to the UK in the 1960s, more recent arrivals and second and third generation women born in the UK to Pakistani and Bangladeshi parents. Some women from poor families in Bangladesh and Pakistan have no formal education, whilst other women have been educated in England, with some leaving full time education at 16 with no or few qualifications and others achieving at postgraduate level (Wigfield 2007).

Adults of Pakistani and Bangladeshi origin of all ages and occupations are least likely to take part in learning, especially those in manual occupations (Aldridge *et al.* 2008). When we examine the statistics relating to women and learning (Aldridge *et al.* 2008) we see clearly that Pakistani, Bangladeshi and Somali women are the least likely group to study. Only 42 per cent of Pakistani women and 34 per cent of Bangladeshi women took part in learning in 2006. This is the lowest participation rate of any group, and in comparison with the highest, 71 per cent of Black African women, is woefully low.

Pakistani, Bangladeshi and Somali adults are most likely to have no qualifications and least likely to have higher level qualifications. Only 18 per cent of Pakistani and 12 per cent of Bangladeshi adults have NVQ Level 4 and above compared with 29 per cent for all respondents. The Labour Force Survey data from 2000 to 2004 indicates similar trends for Somali women. This data indicates that only 2.8 per cent of Somalis have a qualification, although it must be viewed with caution as the sample is very small. Kyambi (2005) found, using LFS and census data, that Somalis constituted the largest proportion of new immigrants to the UK without qualifications (50.1 per cent).

Encouragingly, there are indications of a growing trend for Asian women born in England to become graduates, although their numbers are still small compared to women from other groups. Joseph Rowntree Foundation research (2007) into higher education amongst South Asian women, for instance, discovered that Pakistani women's participation in higher education is moderate and growing rapidly whilst for Bangladeshi women; it is low but still growing rapidly. Nevertheless, Bangladeshi women are still less likely to apply and get in to university.

Research shows that marital status has a significant effect on learning for all groups. This is more pronounced in the Pakistani and Bangladeshi populations where married or cohabiting adults are much less likely to be participating in learning than their single peers. Their participation rates are also significantly lower than those of single and married adults amongst all respondents (Aldridge *et al.* 2008).

Employment

According to a study of barriers to employment for Pakistanis and Bangladeshis in Britain (Tackey *et al.* 2006) and our own analysis of Labour Force Survey data (July to September 2007), Pakistani and Bangladeshi women are the least likely of any group to undertake paid work. Only 21 per cent of Pakistani and 24 per cent of Bangladeshi women are in paid employment (LFS data 2007). High levels of unemployment amongst Somali women are also identified in recent Labour Force Survey data.

The research reveals differences in employment patterns relating to factors such as age and education. Tackey *et al.* (2006) found differences relating to education, qualifications, employment histories and child-rearing expectations. Younger women and second generation women in general value gaining an education or pursuing a career before they have children, and second generation women often have more flexibility about when they start a family. According to Tackey *et al.* (2006) attitudes to work also differ between men and women. Women tend to see employment as a means towards financial independence whereas men want to ensure that they are the breadwinners. Young Bangladeshi women in particular view working positively and as a means of financial independence.

A study from 2006 explored the aspirations of Pakistani, Bangladeshi and Black Caribbean women in employment (Botcherby 2006). Its findings suggest that once in work, Pakistani and Bangladeshi women are often just as ambitious as White British women, if not more so. The majority of women in each of the groups were willing to study for additional qualifications, undertake training or take on extra responsibilities to achieve promotion. However, minority ethnic women in the sample were 3 or 4 times more likely than White British women to have taken a job at a lower level than they were qualified for. Similarly, research into the Somali community found that Somali men were more likely to be working than women and that Somali people who were employed before coming to the UK are likely to be employed in a lower grade occupation (Bloch and Atfield 2002).

Astor *t al.*'s (2007) study into Pakistani and Bangladeshi women's attitudes to work and family identified a strong link between educational background and women's employment experiences. Women with qualifications work in administrative roles such as in the health sector, customer service roles, childcare, classroom assistants or nursery nurses or community roles. Employed women with children consciously fit their work around their childcare responsibilities and so often work part time, in flexible roles or perhaps in roles for which they are actually over qualified. A number of women undertook voluntary work, usually those with fluent English.

Lack of English has a powerful effect on employment prospects. The evidence indicates that without English language, migrants are more likely to be unemployed or concentrated in low paid and low skilled work (Ward 2007). Studies such as Yeandle *et al.* (2006) and Tackey *et al.* (2006) concluded that their biggest barrier to employment is lack of or poor English language skills:

> *"The majority of people interviewed had low levels of education and qualifications, low levels of confidence, limited experience of different types of jobs, and limited networks of contacts in different sectors. At the root of the low level of human capital they possessed was the lack of facility in the English language"*

> Tackey *et al.* 2006, pp. 7–8).

Influences on participation in learning

The influences on participation amongst Bangladeshi, Pakistani and Somali women cited are similar for learning and employment. Two sets of factors appear to influence, and in some cases determine, women's participation and progress in the labour market and in learning. The first relates to women's circumstances and includes factors such as marital status, caring and domestic duties and attitudes. The second relates to educational provision and the ways in which it can either include or exclude marginalised groups.

In relation to the influence of personal circumstances on participation in learning, studies reveal very different patterns of personal, family and community attitudes and support offered to Pakistani, Bangladeshi and Somali daughters and wives in relation to education. Thus, as in the wider population, it is impossible to attribute any one attitude or set of attitudes to these communities. Yeandle *et al.*'s study of ethnic minority women and access to the labour market makes a very useful point in relation to expectations:

"In the women's accounts, parental, family and cultural influences could be positive and negative – encouraging, directing or holding women back. Even with the same local community, cultural and family expectations associated with a woman's role in the home and at work varied greatly, and cannot be generalised along ethnic lines" (2006, p.30).

Research indicates that husbands and families are still very influential in the life choices of girls and women and appears to concur that attitudes are changing (Wigfield 2007, p.25). In her study of South Asian women's lives and struggles, Amrit Wilson (2006) notes that gender relations have undergone a process of transformation over the past 30 years. In Britain, she argues, Asian women's individual and collective struggles against patriarchal control have helped bring about this change. It is now more common for women to work outside the home for instance, and some women have more equal relationships where domestic tasks are shared.

'In this context it is becoming more acceptable for girls and women to remain in education or engage in learning, but there is much variation within this overall trend, much as one would imagine in the wider population (Aston *et al.* 2007; Crozier *et al.* 2004; Dale *et al.* 2000). Some women have the freedom and aspirations to pursue higher education and high-level professional careers (Aston *et al.* 2007; Joseph Rowntree Foundation 2007; Tyrer & Ahmad 2006). Additional reasons for these changes include wider societal changes, greater recognition of education as a means to higher standards of living and the expectations and influence of children raised and educated in the UK.

For other women, attitudes to learning and work cannot be easily distinguished from gender-bound expectations and perceptions of women's role and purpose in life as domestic workers, wives, carers, and mothers. Research based on focus groups with representatives from all the major minority ethnic groups in the UK (Hall *et al.* 2004) concluded that this is still more likely amongst Pakistani and Bangladeshi women than other groups. Wilson (2006) also found that husbands or families frequently continue to expect their wives to carry out most of the domestic labour and childcare in the family home. A minority are subjected to domestic violence and other oppressive behaviour and, she suggests, brides from the sub-continent are "among the most oppressed and exploited daughters in law (p.28). One result of this is that women are preventing from attending classes and learning English because their domestic role is prioritised or, as research such as Aston *et al.* (2007) suggests, some fathers and husbands believe it could give women too much independence and power.

Dale *et al.* (2000) found in their research based on group discussions with Pakistani and Bangladeshi young people in Oldham in education and in employment that parental pressure can be strong; for some young people it meant that they stayed in education when they would have preferred to leave, whilst others' parents were not keen on their daughters remaining in education. Parental concern about the impact of western values on their daughter's behaviour and moral development can influence their choice of secondary school and the kinds of extra curricular activity they permit their daughters to undertake (Crozier *et al.* 2004; Dale *et al.* 2000).

Views on post 16 educations also vary. Most families are supportive, although a minority of fathers expressed reservations about the necessity of post 16 education for their daughters (Crozier *et al.* 2004). As noted above, marriage is associated with a reduction in women's access to learning (Aldridge *et al.* 2008). This can be disproportionate for Pakistani and Bangladeshi women where marriage is the norm and females usually assume that they will get married (Aston *et al.* 2007). According to Labour Force Survey data (July to September 2007), the highest proportion of adults who are married with dependent children are Asian and British Asian; 59 per cent compared to 30 per cent in the White population.

Aston *et al.* (2007) found that there can be great deal of pressure on young women to marry instead of undertaking education or pursuing a career. Amongst the women they interviewed there was an almost universal desire to marry. However, many of these young women hoped to either complete their education or have some employment experience before marriage, often with family support (Aston *et al.* 2007). Family attitudes are not the only determinant of participation. Schools are influential, but not always positive. A research study into Asian women and higher education found that schools did not necessarily see higher education as a natural progression for young Asian women. Indeed, some interviewees felt that their teachers were racist; openly assuming they were destined for marriage and motherhood rather than education or careers (JRF 2007).

Amongst the married women interviewed by Aston *et al.* (2007), some younger women who were recently married had husbands who encouraged them to participate in courses or learn new skills. These women were more likely to continue studying or working until they started a family. Higher qualified women were more likely to share domestic tasks with their husbands. In contrast, first generation women who had migrated to the UK years ago were simply expected to be 'good' wives and mothers, in other words to concentrate on their home and family.

Studies have concluded that younger second or third generation women, those born and raised in the UK, are likely to have more independence and different expectations than first generation women who came to the UK for marriage, (Aston *et al.* 2007; Tackey *et al.* 2006). Joseph Rowntree Foundation (2007) and Aston *et al.* (2007) found that marriage, although pivotal in the plans of young Bangladeshi and Pakistani women, is not necessarily a deterrent to higher education. Some had negotiated with their families to defer marriage until they completed their studies, but they found it harder to gain agreement to leave home to study, and local universities were usually the preference of parents and the wider community, a finding also noted by Crozier *et al.* (2004) and Dale *et al.* (2000).

There is little research on the Somali community in the UK and their cultural or family expectations of men and women learning. Qualitative research by the Joseph Rowntree Foundation found that social networks of Somali men and women were usually centred on the home or the local Somali community. Somali women, particularly those who were recent arrivals to the UK, were more restricted in their activities: their lives tended to revolve around taking children to and from school, visiting parks, shopping for food and sometimes visiting local Somali family or friends and Somali community centres (Hudson et al. 2007). They concluded that locating access to education within these contexts was an effective approach to widening participation for these women.

Childcare

Childcare responsibilities have a major impact on all women's ability and willingness to access learning and employment. Pakistani, Bangladeshi and Somali women expect to have children and often have large families. It is more prevalent for women from these groups to choose to care for their children themselves when they are young and to prioritise mothering over studying and working (Aston *et al.* 2007). This is through choice and because of the practical challenges entailed in combining caring responsibilities with learning or employment. However, as Tackey et al (2006) observe, this means women with large families can be out of the labour market for long periods of time. The situation is similar for Somali women who regard looking after the family and home as their primary responsibility (Bloch & Atfield 2002). In contrast, research by Hall et al (2004) found that White, Black African, Black Caribbean and Chinese women were more likely to employ a childminder.

Where Pakistani and Bangladeshi women do access childcare, there is a tendency to prefer informal childcare arrangements using family, and many are reluctant to use childminders and other formal arrangements (Aston *et al.* 2007; Hall *et al.* 2004; Tackey *et al.* 2006). Similarly, Atubo & Batterby (2001) observed that Somali women prefer their children to be cared for by another Somali woman. This presents a barrier to engaging in learning or work where family are not willing or able to care for their children. The Labour Force Survey (July to September 2007) indicates that almost half the Somali women surveyed are female lone parents with dependent children. Arguably it may be harder for women without a partner to access learning, especially if they prefer to use family childcare as this relies on their availability and goodwill. Further significant barriers to using formal childcare, as for all women, are cost and inflexibility, especially absence of provision for school holidays (Hall *et al.* 2004).

Domestic responsibilities

Other domestic and caring responsibilities can act as additional barriers to participation in learning and employment. There is an expectation in many families that women will take sole or joint responsibility for caring for elderly or sick family members or in laws (Aston *et al.* 2007; Hall *et al.* 2004; Tackey *et al.* 2006). This can be a further obstacle to participation in learning or employment. Yeandle et al (2006) found that the proportions of Pakistani and Bangladeshi women of working age who provide unpaid care is higher than in other groups; for example, in Camden, 11% of Bangladeshi women and 5% of Pakistani women had demanding caring responsibilities compared with 2.5% of White British women.

Hall *et al.* (2004) and White & Weaver (2007) concluded that the practicalities of being a wife and mother mean that it can be more feasible for a woman to stay at home and raise her children rather than trying to balance, and afford, employment with childcare. Aston *et al.* (2007) noted the different outlooks on this, with a tendency for first generation wives to expect to take total responsibility for domestic duties and second and third generation and more educated women expecting to share household tasks with their husbands, although, again, actual situations varied. Domestic labour is time consuming and can make fitting in classes, especially if they require travelling some distance, too difficult or impractical.

Confidence

The theme of confidence, or lack of it, emerged in some of the literature looking at Bangladeshi and Pakistani women's' experiences of education and employment (see, for example, Tackey *et al.* 2006; Aston *et al.* 2007; BEAP 2004). Lack of confidence can be a barrier for women from all ethnic groups, but can be exacerbated by other factors such as isolation, fear of family or community disapproval and racism. Yeandle *et al.* highlighted this in relation to paid employment, noting that particularly amongst recent immigrant women, "overcoming fear, isolation and depression and gaining the confidence to do something new was a re-current theme" (2006, p.27).

Under developed English language skills can generate lack of confidence. In turn this can then prove to be a barrier for some women to participating in learning or employment. As one study noted, in its suggestion that learning provision needs to be local, some women do not feel able to travel to access learning and "clearly lacked confidence to leave their immediate familiar surroundings" (Wigfield 2007, p.52).

The hindrances to Bangladeshi, Pakistani and Somali women's participation in learning identified in this section are not unique. On the contrary, as McGivney (2001) notes in her work on widening adult participation in learning, the way in which psychological, cultural, structural and practical factors such as those outlined above limit adults' participation in learning is widely known and understood. What is absent from the research literature, is an explanation of why, if these factors are common to all groups, the rates of access to learning for Pakistani, Bangladeshi and Somali women are significantly and consistently lower. English language might have a significant influence and we will now discuss access to English language teaching and the impact this can have on lives and learning.

English language

Enhancing English language proficiency can help women to build a firm foundation for tackling oppression, discrimination and inequalities in their lives because English language is one of the multiple factors that affect the well-being, prosperity, economic advancement and settlement of migrants (NIACE 2006). Ability to use English underpins autonomy and independence and raises self-esteem. It has wider social benefits including raised aspirations, improved health, increased access to services, more opportunities for civic, democratic and community participation and activism (O' Leary 2008, Schuller *et al.* 2004, Ward 2007).

Pakistani and Bangladeshi women have the lowest English language levels of all the major ethnic groups (Tackey *et al.* 2006). According to this research, only 4 per cent of Bangladeshi and 28 per cent of Pakistani women aged 45-64 speak fluent English. These women do not join learning provision for a number of reasons that include gender oppression, family circumstances and a lack of time, independence and control. Structural inadequacies especially lack of childcare, provision too far from home, no women only classes for women who need them, non-flexible or poorly timed provision or simple lack of information about where to find it can also prevent these women accessing learning (Ward 2007). Learning organisations, faced with overwhelming demand from newly arrived migrants, have had little incentive to seek out more students when their classes are already bursting (Dalziel & Sofres 2005; NIACE 2006).

Questions about the quality and appropriacy of provision have been raised in the research literature. Recent changes in migration patterns have led to huge increases in demand, and more diverse student populations with multiple and complex learning interests and needs. The NIACE Committee of Inquiry which investigated English for Speakers of Other Languages (ESOL) in England (NIACE 2006) concluded that notwithstanding many examples of responsive provision and creative teaching and learning, there are enormous challenges in ESOL which need urgent attention. Demand has outstripped supply, there is insufficient funding, the content of learning does not always align with learner demand, the quality is variable and in many areas there are huge difficulties recruiting and training ESOL teachers. Similar challenges were identified in a recent study of ESOL needs in London (O'Leary 2008).

Funding

The state has funded English language learning (ESOL) for many years, and the Learning and Skills Council is the primary source of ESOL funding. Despite increases in overall funding, from £103 million in 2001-2 to over £300 million in 2007-8, the funding allocated by the government is insufficient to provide free ESOL for all who need it. When considering a solution to this dilemma, the government decided not to expand ESOL funding, but to reprioritise public funds towards those deemed to be most in need and encourage contributions to the cost of learning from learners and employers.

Changes to ESOL funding arrangements introduced in September 2007 include the introduction of fees, with remission for learners in receipt of means tested benefit, and the removal of the right of asylum seekers over the age of 19 to access ESOL unless they have not received a decision on their application after 6 months or are unable to leave for reasons beyond their control. A hardship fund was introduced for 2007-8 following the outcomes of a Race Equality Impact Assessment of the proposed reforms (DfES 2007) where respondents stressed that the proposed changes could make asylum seekers and women unable to access family income or evidence of entitlement to fees remission vulnerable to exclusion. Although the data to support assessment of the impact of the changes are not yet available, Pakistani, Bangladeshi and Somali women are likely to be highly represented in this group. At the time of writing the continuation of the Hardship Fund safety net has yet to be confirmed

Recently arrived spouses also have to wait at least one year to gain eligibility for state funded ESOL provision. Research by Kofman *et al.* (2005) into gender and migration demonstrates that migration to join spouses or fiancées in the UK is predominantly female and the highest numbers are from Pakistan and Bangladesh. Data on their ability to speak English are not available, but it is reasonable to assume that proficiency in English varies and some have an urgent need to learn. In the period they are not eligible for provision they may start families and/or enter the labour market and this can delay, often indefinitely, their take up of language classes. Research into effective teaching and learning (Baynham *et al.* 2007) demonstrates both the outstanding economic and social benefits of learning English for settlement and the detrimental effects of delays in starting to learn on progress and achievement. Unpublished research[15] into the impact of the funding changes carried out by NIACE indicate that a substantial amount of the Entry Levels 1 and 2[16] provision most likely to be accessed by these groups has disappeared which suggests that inclusion is receding in many places rather than expanding.

---

15. NIACE impact assessment survey carried out behalf of DIUS (unpublished)
16. Entry level is the first level of the National Qualifications Framework. It lies beneath level 1 and is subdivided into three levels – 1, 2 and 3, with 3 being the highest. These sub-levels are broadly comparable with national curriculum levels 1, 2 and 3. Visit the QCA website for more information: http://www.qca.org.uk/qca_5780.aspx

Family learning

Family learning can be a powerful gateway to learning. It offers safe and accessible environments in which mothers and other carers can develop their own skills, understanding and knowledge at the same time as enriching their approaches to supporting their children's education (Rees *et al.* 2003).

Attracting women into learning that equips them to support their children's education is especially important in the light of the findings of a study into the intergenerational effects of mothers' education on their children's school achievements (Carneiro *et al.* 2006). This work concluded that the level of the mother's education is one of the most significant influences on children's achievements. Data produced by the then Department for Education and Skills indicate that mothers of Asian pupils, especially Bangladeshi pupils, are the most likely to have no qualifications; eighty-five per cent of mothers of Bangladeshi pupils and almost 70 per cent of Pakistani mothers had no qualifications compared to only 16 per cent of White British mothers (DfES 2006). This is likely to be a contributory factor to the findings of the same report that children from Pakistani, Bangladeshi and Somali backgrounds consistently perform below the average for all pupils on every scale, and achieve poor GCSE results

There is huge potential in Early Year's services to recruit excluded women to learning such as language provision and learning associated with young children. Sure Start, the national Early Year's programme that works with families with young children in disadvantaged areas, has potential to offer a valuable contribution. It does so in some places, but an evaluation of Sure Start and black and minority ethnic populations carried out by Craig *et al.* in 2007 found a very uneven picture. There were examples of good practice in engaging local Asian families, but the overall conclusion was that, "The treatment of ethnicity as a dimension in the work of Sure Start was fragmented, partial or lacking altogether" (p.3) resulting in the exclusion of marginalised minority ethnic families. The report concluded that, 'There is a need most of all for some very strong guidance on understanding difference and diversity and the implications of this for service delivery' (p. 9).

Research has shown that parents are almost always highly supportive of their children's education, but the help they can offer their children is often limited by lack of knowledge and understanding of the educational system. Crozier *et al.* (2004) and Dale *et al.* (2000) have shown that this can be varied depending on their own social background, level of education and experience of the UK education system. These studies found that parents who had not been educated in the UK, who had limited or no educational qualifications and little English were the most disadvantaged, especially as information from the school was rarely translated.

Family learning can assist parents, carers and school staff to develop greater understanding of each others' expectations and overcome misunderstandings based on differing cultural expectations of the roles of schools, teachers and parents that are identified in studies such as Gregory (2006). Employing staff from diverse backgrounds can aid intercultural dialogue and understanding, and family learning can enthuse women to consider working in schools as teachers or classroom assistants. This not only enhances their own career prospects but these staff can then act as role models to other women and pupils, enlarge and enrich cultural perspectives in schools and help to foster positive relationships between parents, schools and communities (Ward 2007).

Provision for learners with little literacy

Many of the Pakistani, Bangladeshi and Somali women most excluded from learning have lower levels of education and little or no literacy in any language. In their study of effective practice in ESOL, Baynham *et al.* (2007) found that it is virtually impossible to satisfy all learners' diverse needs in very mixed classes, and conclude that different types of provision are essential to support learning and progress for all. Learners with higher levels of education often benefit from fast track or intensive courses. Those with few or no written literacy skills in any language and little history of schooling, often Pakistani, Bangladeshi and Somali women, have significant and complex learning needs. In general, they make slower progress and can require more intensive and specialist support to help them make progress and stay the course (Baynham *et al.* 2007). These needs are not always recognised or addressed in generic, mixed level ESOL programmes. The same study concluded that their difficulties can be compounded where they have been settled in the UK for some time, as long-term residents tend to make slower progress than recent arrivals.

Funding allocations and targets tied to achievement of national targets at Entry level 3, Level 1 and Level 2 also serve to exclude those with the least experience of education. In their evidence to the NIACE Committee of Inquiry, ESOL teachers and managers expressed deep disquiet about the consequences for learners below Entry level 3 where ESOL at this level is diminishing as local funding allocations prioritise achievements at Entry levels 1 and 2 to meet Public Service Agreement (PSA) Targets (NIACE 2006). This narrowing of opportunities can have profound consequences as research offers a powerful and consistent message that adults with language skills below Level 1 are likely to experience the highest levels of social injustice, and the most difficulties in securing sustainable employment, accessing services and participating in their communities (Ward 2007).

Community participation

Community participation and cohesion is a policy area with implications for Pakistani, Bangladeshi and Somali women. Community cohesion as a concept has risen up the government policy agenda in recent years, initially sparked by the 'disturbances' in Northern towns in 2001 and fuelled by concerns about terrorism in Muslim communities following 9/11 and the London bombings (JRF 2008). Policy solutions are formulated in terms of promoting Britishness, citizenship, integration and community cohesion (Home Office 2005a, 2005b, Commission for Integration and Cohesion 2007).

These concepts are problematic and are not universally understood in the same way. Researchers have observed that community cohesion is often focused on minority ethnic groups, especially Muslims, rather than whole communities (Zetter *et al.* 2006; JRF 2008). As Zetter *et al* put it in their study of immigration, social cohesion and social capital; community policy tends to be directed to the immigrant communities:

"In short, while immigrant communities remain in the spotlight, it is neither evident what it is they might be cohering to, nor clear who is, or should be, doing the cohering"

(Zetter et al. 2006, p.8)

Research into members' perceptions of their communities reveals a more nuanced picture of Asian and Somali views on community. A number of studies find many positive community elements in areas where the majority of residents are from the same ethnic group (Cole & Robinson 2003; Hudson *et al.* 2007; JRF 2008; Robinson *et al.* 2007; Simpson *et al.* 2007). These are often thriving neighbourhoods where residents feel safe, are close to family and friendship networks and have easy access to community support networks and local services and amenities such as mosques and shops selling Halal food. In their study of race, housing and community cohesion in Oldham and Rochdale, Simpson *et al.* (2007) conclude that this type of clustering in a geographical area is not necessarily negative.

> *"Racial clustering of this nature is no more worrying than clustering that separates social classes and tenure types into observable residential cluster"*

(page 8)

A different perspective is offered by research into the housing aspirations of white and second generation South Asian British women (Harries *et al.* 2008). This study found that, as above, both groups of women prioritised features such as safety and good schools and amenities. However, the second generation South Asian women differed from their mothers in that they often wanted to live away from areas with high concentrations of their ethnic group which they perceived as 'constrictive and intrusive'.

Another finding of research into community is that many Asian and Somali migrants living on mixed estates experience racism, harassment and anti social behaviour, especially in disadvantaged areas. In their study of Somali women in West London, Atubo & Batterby (2001) found that the women felt unsafe and often encountered hostility or aggression from other residents, for example, because they wore traditional dress.

Unsurprisingly, these experiences are a major deterrent to residency in these types of neighbourhoods as well as a hindrance to community cohesion (Atubo & Batterby 2001; Cole & Robinson 2003; JRF 2008).

Recent research carried out into Muslim communities concluded that racial and religious discrimination are key barriers to developing a sense of belonging in Britain (JRF 2008). This study found evidence of informal interaction between different groups in their everyday life, especially for women in the middle age range, born in the UK, educated to secondary level, employed or students, with family responsibilities and fluent in English. It concludes from this that this challenges common perceptions of economically inactive Muslim women as isolated from wider society. At the same time, the profile of the active women indicates that women with the least education and lowest language levels are the most likely to be excluded. The research also noted that in spite of concern about local problems such as crime and drug use, there are low levels of participation in local organisations aiming to tackle these problems especially amongst women caring for families. Reasons cited were lack of time, feeling unwelcome, lack of relevance to their lives, and negative attitudes within their community to women's participation in local organisations. Insufficient English is a contributory element.

English language is identified by government as vital for community cohesion (Commission for Integration and Cohesion 2007; DIUS 2008). A citizenship test has been introduced in which applicants for citizenship have to demonstrate competence in English as well as knowledge of life in the UK. The government has recently consulted on proposals to focus ESOL on community cohesion (DIUS 2008). The consultation document appears to conflate English language, a vital condition for community cohesion, with community cohesion itself. As studies such as Atubo & Batterby (2001), Cole & Robinson (2003), and JRF (2008) clearly demonstrate, English language is rarely the sole cause of divided communities. It is important, but usually one of a number of multiple factors affecting community interaction and engagement. It follows, therefore, that to be effective, solutions need to address this complexity.

The NIACE response to the ESOL and community cohesion consultation (DIUS 2008) called on the government to sharpen the conceptualisation and language relating to social inclusion, community cohesion and the role of ESOL. There must be recognition of how much the roots of exclusion lie in poverty, racism, fear of difference, inequitable housing policies and inequalities of power and resources, both within communities and wider society as this will help to formulate solutions founded on a recognition of the challenges that need to be tackled to make a real difference. These will need to include all members of communities not just those without proficiency, in English because to concentrate on this group could intensify divisions (NIACE 2008). The JRF (2008) study also stressed the part that local organisations, including learning centres and ESOL classes play in bringing people together.

Summary

It is clear from the literature that it is not helpful to refer to Bangladeshi, Pakistani and Somali women as though they are a homogeneous group. There are huge differences in the life chances and attainments of women from these groups. Age is a significant determinant and there is evidence that many younger women who were born or grew up in Britain have more chance of entering higher education and professional careers. However, they are doing so in lower numbers than their peers from different ethnic groups. At the other end of the scale we see that Bangladeshi, Pakistani and Somali women with little education or fluency in English are highly likely to be living in poverty with little access to well paid employment. They are significantly under represented in adult learning, one of the major routes to autonomy, economic advancement and intergenerational achievement. We now turn to the question of why many women from these groups do not access learning. The next section explores the circumstances and views of Bangladeshi, Pakistani and Somali women who are not participating in organised learning.

4. Women not participating in organised learning

The women we interviewed ranged in ages from 17 to over 70. The majority of the Bangladeshi and Pakistani women came to England either as children to join their families or as adults to join husbands or fiancées. Eleven were born or grew up in the UK. The Somali women had mostly arrived as refugees fleeing the civil war. Some had lived in another European county, primarily the Netherlands, Sweden and Denmark, before moving to the UK to join other family members. The women's life histories, education backgrounds, levels of English, economic circumstances, employment situations and family and marital relationships differed enormously. A small minority were subjected to abuse and oppression, whilst the life patterns and choices of others were largely determined by their gender, albeit to different degrees. All these factors, in different combinations, influenced their educational opportunities.

Our conversations with 100 Pakistani, Bangladeshi and Somali women, 62 of whom were not taking part in organised education, revealed the diversity and complexities of their lives, identities and relationships with their families and communities. Their backgrounds, experiences and responses to them vary and there are often tensions and contradictions within their own lives and identities. Happy, fulfilled lives contrast with those of drudgery and abuse. The security of warm, loving families and friendship and support networks in close-knit communities is set against isolation and gender oppression of various degrees within families and discrimination and racism outside them. Although only a small minority claim equal relationships with their husbands, many of the women are able to decide for themselves whether they work and/or learn. In contrast, seven of the women have virtually no autonomy and are subservient to the demands of their husband or family.

Common threads weave through their differences, not least the desire for independence, although attainment of this differs. English language and access to learning opportunities are among the keys to this independence as well as other features of the 'good lives' the women aspire to. Access to learning is explored in the following sections: learning histories, attitudes to learning, English language fluency and aspirations, barriers to learning, employment and community involvement.

Learning histories

We investigated the women's schooling as this can influence their learning experiences as adults. A few of the women had never been to school, others had attended primary and secondary school and a small number were university or college graduates. Access to schooling in childhood was associated with a number of factors that included country, family income, urban or rural upbringing and family and cultural attitudes to education. Women who grew up in towns and cities tended to have higher levels of school education. In general, women from poor rural backgrounds in Bangladesh, Pakistan and Somalia had limited experience of education, primarily because of poor economic circumstances and cultural expectations that constrained the roles of girls and women.

Economic circumstances

Poverty frequently prevented girls getting an education, either because families could not afford schooling or it was not available, especially in villages. Girls who attended primary school were often unable to continue because of their families could not afford the high fees or transport costs. Moreover, boys' education was prioritised to prepare them for their future role as breadwinners.

Nusrat described the impact of poverty on educational opportunities in the village she left at the age of nine:

'I come from a small village in Pakistan. It is a little village which is full of poor people who live in very small houses where life is extremely difficult because the jobs there are really low paid and the work is hard labour whatever you do. There is no government fund, the people are not fortunate in terms of wealth and therefore education is not an option.'

Daughters were married as young as possible in families like Halima's because they could not afford to keep them at home:

'I had to help around the house with my other sisters because we lost our father when we were very small. We all sisters got married at a very young age because we had no income and were finding it very hard to cope with daily survival. Being in this situation we had no luck to be taught basic skills let alone have education.'

Most of the women described growing up in communities where home making and child rearing were viewed as their primary purpose in life and education of little relevance to their future.

'My family don't value education and that's the reason why they thought it would be best for me to marry as I was at home doing nothing. My mother never had an education and she has always been illiterate and never saw the use of girls and education because girls always end up married and as a housewife. My mother thought it was more important that girls should learn how to sew and cook.' (Mrs Begum)

Educating girls also carried the danger of exposing families to the risk of 'losing face' in the community as education might impede their acceptance of their domestic destiny or compromise their modesty. Families were keen to preserve their 'honour' by ensuring that their girls were not seen out alone, even to go to school. Sofia stressed the importance of reputation, honour and respect, saying that families 'do not care about their daughters getting an education but care more about respect in the village'.

Some girls had been encouraged to study, often when their parents were educated or they lived in urban areas. However, restricted educational opportunities in villages, although commonplace, were not universal. Shalina described the high value placed on education in her village in Bangladesh:

'I come from a small village where everyone went to school because this was important in our village. Young children would be visited at home if they were not in school by the age of 5 years. Teachers would go to the homes and ask the parents why the child didn't start yet? ... Our village had strict guidelines to follow and our schools had better success rates overall than most schools in neighbouring villages.'

It was more common for the Somali women to say that their family and communities valued educated women. Women like Nimo and Abshiro remember that their families and communities in Somalia believed that girls' education promoted independence and positive progress for life in the future.

'ilmaha ayay u fiicantahay, kalsooni buuxda ayay siinaysaa, danahooda in ay ku qabsadaan, ...shaqadu waa ka mid – it is good for the children and gives them (women) full confidence.'

The women schooled in the UK benefited from free compulsory education to the age of 16 but their access to opportunities in further and higher education differed, often due to parental attitudes. Some progressed to higher education whilst others were denied opportunities, for example Lubna, a 34 year old woman of Pakistani heritage born in the UK. She completed secondary education but was not allowed by her parents to pursue her ambition to train as a teacher because they believed that young Asian girls should get married at an early age and concentrate on becoming housewives.

Women's access to learning

Culturally determined concepts of women's roles within family life are a very powerful determinant of their access to education as adults. Unsurprisingly, we discovered a broad spectrum of aspirations, attitudes and views on the value of women's learning amongst the women, their families and communities; we found inconsistencies and contradictions as well as common trends. Aspirations and views are shaped by a combination of early experiences and family, social, cultural and economic circumstances and have often modified over time. Other crucial influences are expectations, age, domestic circumstances, whether the women were born here or have recently migrated to the UK and the attitudes and behaviour of husbands and in-laws. Inevitably the following is a snapshot of views rather than a definitive representation of attitudes to learning in all families and communities. It does, however, provide insights into the ways in which concepts of family and women's role are very influential determinants of attitudes towards learning.

Women's attitudes

'If you do not learn English you are not here.' (Ghazala)

Every woman we spoke to recognises the value of adult learning, especially English language. Women of all ages, whether currently learning or not, are convinced of the value of education for girls and women as well as boys and men. They see it as essential for understanding and living successfully in UK society, for independence, for securing good jobs, to set an example for their children and to give them high aspirations. English is associated with status and treatment by others:

'People have no time for you if you have no English.' (Leyla)

'Education is what makes the world go round. Without education there would be no doctors to save lives, there'd be no hospitals for all the sick people.' (Nusrat)

'Learning is like a light.' (Shamso)

'Learning looks like an eye. If you don't have an eye you don't see what is happening around you.' (Shara)

Without exception the women we interviewed have high aspirations for their children and believe their daughters should have the same educational opportunities as their sons, including university education. Several reported with pride that their sons and daughters have degrees and professional careers:

'I am especially proud of my daughter who studied very well and managed to work and look after her husband and his family and took care of her own children too.' (Mrs. Khanom)

However, women who see the importance of their children's education do not necessarily think of learning for themselves and often prioritise homemaking and family life.

Family and community attitudes

The married women live either with their husbands and children or in extended families with husbands, children, parents in law and sometimes their husband's other siblings. Attitudes towards women's education and levels of support offered by husbands and in-laws are a significant factor in whether women access learning. These range from encouragement and support to active opposition. Women are often encouraged by their families and communities to take up learning opportunities although, as we see in the next section, other factors then prevent them from doing so.

A small number, seven, of the women have very low status in their family hierarchy. They live, or have lived in the past, in oppressive circumstances in which they are dominated and controlled by their husbands and often their in-laws. They have no choice about what happens in their lives, are forbidden to leave the house without permission and are not allowed to learn English. This is usually related to the imposition of sole responsibility for domestic labour in the household, overt intention to deny any independence, and fears of damaging the husband's 'honour', for example if the woman mixes with men outside or attends a mixed class.

Iram describes why her dreams to study art were thwarted:

'The cultural manner towards the situation is that a woman should not be officially recognised to work or study. Her duty is to stay at home and look after her family home and her family. Her duties are to cook for the whole family and have a high opinion of her husband to respect and obey his decision and honour him.'

Even where families and community members are generally supportive, learning is usually sanctioned only if the children and housework take precedence. Mothers are expected to ensure that home life is taken care of, and may only engage in education if that life isn't adversely affected. Arguably this may well be the case in many white British families too. Some women are refused any help and burdened with full responsibility. This means they cannot find time to attend English classes or have no childcare to enable them to attend.

The women who are learning usually live in supportive family situations where their husbands or other female family members encourage them and sometimes look after the children to enable them to study. Some husbands insist their wives learn English to make their lives easier or because, like Shara's husband, they prefer educated women. Mariam's husband is also learning English and they have agreed a shift system where one studies in the morning and the other does childcare then they swap for the afternoon. The parents of the young women who access learning encourage and support them. Almost without exception the women said that their children encouraged them to learn English for more independence and reduce their reliance on their children to interpret for them.

External opinions have a profound influence on some of the women and their families, whereas others are less concerned about others' judgements. Women such as Sofia live in environments where community members encourage them to learn English and try to put pressure on husbands who prevent their wives from learning. Alternatively, anxiety about negative judgement deters women such as Atharjan, who stopped attending classes because she feared the stigma of people thinking she was not a good mother, and Hamida who started to learn English ten years ago but then left because she thought people were gossiping about her. Other women are more resistant to this kind of pressure. They say the community has no right to make choices for them and are prepared to ignore or resist those who try to exert their views on them:

> *'I have to live for myself and stand up for myself to live in this world.' (Aruj)*

Changing attitudes

One of the prevailing themes revealed by the women is that attitudes are changing. While the attitudes of some are fossilised in the past, we consistently heard that mindsets are altering and women themsleves, their families and communities are becoming more positive about the education of women. Women such as Leyla, for example, used to think that she should care for her children first but her views have now changed and she would like to learn as she realises that 'Without education you are nothing'. At the same time, this is not yet universal, and there is a general view that older people and those from villages are slower to change

The women suggest the reasons for this are shifting societal norms, pressure from women and the example and influence of children. Lubna, for instance, told us with great satisfaction that she has persuaded her parents to change their views on women and education so that her two younger sisters are now at university. The experiences of children growing up in the UK are influentiall as educated and successful children are opening the eyes of others in their communities to the realisation that education is important to success. This is accompanied by an increasing general awareness of the importance of education to securing 'decent' employment and gaining a good standard of living.

Attitudes to whether women should learn and their sometimes restrictive conditions are a significant determinant of whether they do actually engage in learning. We will explore this in more detail in the next section with particular emphasis on learning English.

Sofia's story

"My husband says 'there is no point in me learning English when I am going to spend the rest of my entire life looking after his children and his family'"

Sofia came to the UK as a 16 year old bride. Now aged 22, she lives in Blackburn, Lancashire with her husband, their two children and her mother and father-in-law. She is fluent in Punjabi but can only speak a few English expressions although she understands a lot more. This means that when she visits places where English is spoken she has to take someone with her to translate. However, her husband works nights and her mother and father-in-law cannot speak English so she is reliant on neighbours to help her.

Sofia has a strong drive to learn English and would love to go to college. Her local community are very positive and encouraging about women learning English and working: "They say, 'It's fantastic knowing how to speak English and getting from place to place with no problems at all'". Despite her thirst to learn, Sofia's family environment is oppressive and she is not allowed to leave the house without permission from her husband and mother-in-law. Her husband is adamant that she doesn't need to learn English and remains steadfast in his opposition even though neighbours have attempted to persuade him to relent.

Sofia's expectations have changed. On moving to the UK she decided that learning English was crucial if she wanted to get a job. But sadly, sharing this hope with her husband made him angry. "He shattered my dreams of learning English and gaining self-confidence. This made me very distressed and disappointed and I learnt not to make any decision without asking my husband first". Sofia hopes that her two sons are able to access as much education as possible and feels that the cultural outlook for boys means that is possible.

Learning English

We examine access to learning English as English language is crucial to women gaining more independence and access to greater social and economic inclusion. Fourteen of the women not in education had never accessed learning as adults in the UK. Other women had learned English and/or other subjects in the past but stopped. Reasons for this were often marriage, pregnancy and the birth of their children when family attitudes, shortage of time or lack of childcare became barriers to accessing learning. Others gave up because they were unhappy with the teaching, because of illness or lack of transport or in one case no progression or information, advice and guidance offered when the course finished, demonstrating how easily people can slip through the net without timely and appropriate information, advice and guidance and follow up work to support women to persist with their learning.

Five of the Pakistani women and six of the Bangladeshi women are fluent in English as they were born or brought up in the UK. The language levels of the other women range from women who have virtually no spoken or written English to a woman who describes her English as level 3[17]. The language levels of women not in learning are noticeably undeveloped. All the Pakistani and Bangladeshi women and half the Somali women in this group had very low levels of English, reporting that they could only write their name, and understand and say very little. The next section explores the impact of proficiency in English on their lives.

---

17. Level 3 is broadly equivalent to A level standard

What women can do

The women who can use English stress that this gives them confidence, freedom and independence, as well as the ability to make judgements and choices.

> *'It's the key of life. If you are in the country without knowing the language you are closed in a cupboard.'*
> *(Zainab)*

The women with little English described getting by and being able to say 'easy things' such as 'hello', 'yes' and 'no'. One response to limited English is to avoid communication with English speakers. In contrast, others use the limited English they do have to communicate as much as possible, for instance greeting neighbours, talking to their children's teachers and health visitors even though these interactions are limited and they cannot have in-depth conversations.

What women struggle to do

Some women do not use English at all, relying on family members to undertake all their English transactions. Whilst some accept this, others find it very restricting. The way in which lack of English robs many of the women of independence and saps their confidence is a strong and recurring theme. This is linked with low self-esteem and timidity, 'you are scared if you can't talk,' and frustration because they can't do things independently.

We heard numerous examples of ways in which little or no English limits what women can do in almost every aspect of their everyday life. They described how it affects their ability to assert their rights, access health care and other services, interact with others in a range of different situations, get involved in their children's education or go outside of the home independently. Some do not feel they can talk to neighbours, answer the door or use the phone. They avoid Sure Start Children's Centre sessions, struggle to talk to teachers and other parents at the school gates, don't take children to the library or read them bedtime stories in English. They cannot use public transport or learn to drive.

Women such as Wakaran regret not having learned English when younger. Her basic English is compounding her struggle to survive as a young widow bringing up her two children and contributes to her severe depression. Khadra 's lack of English prevents her gaining a better understanding of English society, her human rights, and her children's rights:

> *'I feel somewhat blindfolded as I'm not always aware of what I'm entitled to, where I can go to find useful information and improving my English will give me the confidence to find this out.'*

All the women currently in learning referred to the increased confidence and independence they have gained as their ability to communicate and negotiate social situations and contexts has developed. They prize being able to make choices, access services and resolve problems without relying on others to interpret for them.

What women want to do

Almost all the women would like to increase their fluency in English become more confident, independent and less reliant on others thereby improving their day to day life. They view English language as opening up the world to them by liberating them to go out alone, walk in the community, and use public transport. Learning to drive is important to enable them to travel around independently. Sofia who isn't allowed to leave her house would:

'... like to go to college and learn the language then explore the whole of England, go to different towns and cities and get to see the world.'

They want to access health care without having to use interpreters, use services, read and write letters and use the phone, go swimming and take up exercise. The desire to communicate without interpreters was a constant theme. Women said they make best use of their little English but cannot go into depth or understand everything that is said to them. This makes them worried and uneasy and it can be embarrassing when they have to use their children. They stress that they do need interpreters in some situations, if a person is scared, for example when they go into hospital, they can't say anything and need help. One woman described her terror when soon after her arrival she gave birth in a hospital where no-one spoke Gujarati and she couldn't speak or understand any English.

Children are a major stimulus for the women's desire to learn English. They told us that their children are growing up with English as their dominant language so their mothers don't understand them and have difficulty communicating as the children 'speak like water.' All the parents want to be able to attend parents' evenings and talk to their children's teachers about their learning and development in more detail. They want to support their children better, mentioning visits to the library, reading bedtime stories and helping with homework.

'Firstly, I would like to help my children with their homework as I feel so helpless when they ask for my assistance... I want to be able to read them stories. I want to feel confident in speaking with the teachers and going to appointments on my own without having to hassle other people to come and interpret for me. I want to be able to be independent.' (Sofia)

Gaining work, improving career prospects and progressing to further study are important aspirations, although, as we shall see in the section on work, not all women want or are able to work, at least not in the short term. They see English as essential for them to integrate and contribute to the community, know their rights and apply for citizenship. They want to make friends, talk to neighbours and other parents at school, playgroup or the Sure Start Children's Centre:

'When I walk to school some English ladies always say hello to me and even though I would like to stay and chat I can't because of my language barrier so I just say hello back and walk away.' (Anwara)

'It is good to have the knowledge because when people are talking you are not left on your own looking lost and confused' (Raheela)

Barriers to learning

The women faced different barriers to accessing learning. This made some decide not to learn as they can't see how to overcome the obstacles in their way, even though they feel the restrictions that lack of proficiency in English places on their lives. Some women have never been to English classes although some of them have tried to learn informally, helped by family and picking it up from the television but they have made little progress. Others attended classes in the past but stopped when the class ended or when they started their families. Women do make it to classes and progress in learning and the reasons for this will be taken up in the next section. First, this section explores the multiple factors that combined to hinder access to learning for the women in our study.

Attitudinal and cultural

Some women said they have no need for English as their husbands and family have always done everything for them. A number now regret this because they realise they have been denied independence and control over their lives. The consequences can be devastating when life changes such as widowhood or divorce force a woman into circumstances where she has to take responsibility. Wakaran describes how she has been 'in despair' since her husband died because she doesn't know how to manage her everyday life and deal with bills, mail and the mortgage. Nusrat who grew up in the UK had a 'terrible' marriage to a man who would not allow her out of the house. They were divorced after ten years and she is struggling to cope. Depression, arthritis, looking after her children and financial worries all stop her from taking up learning.

The attitudes of the women's immediate families, especially those of husbands and in-laws, explored on pages **36** and **37** have a strong influence on their access to education. A number of the women desperately want to learn English or study other subjects but are forbidden to attend classes by their husbands or in-laws. This is more common in the Pakistani and Bangladeshi families. Only one of the Somali women said she couldn't learn because her husband makes her stay at home.

Women who grew up in the UK can also find themselves in this restrictive position. Nasreen who did not continue her education beyond school now regrets this and would like to study but is not allowed to attend classes by her husband's family who she describes as having a 'village mentality' because they do not believe in women's education.

Women who migrated from Bangladesh and Pakistan to join their husbands from abroad are particularly vulnerable to this control. The stories of the older women show that husbands and in-laws imposing oppressive restrictions on their wives were common in the past. These patterns are not confined to history though, as we see in the stories of women like Sofia (page 38). Shalina from Bangladesh is in a similar position although she retains some fight:

> *'As the years have gone by I am slowly giving up hope of learning and progress because my in laws have given me no hope. There is still a small amount left in me that says go.'*

Fathema arrived at 15 as a bride and her husband prevented her from going to classes because he feared she would start thinking for herself, meet other men, defy his authority and become independent.

Changes to their living situations are one way of escaping these controls. Jahanara couldn't learn English during her first five years in England because she lived with her father in law who would not allow her to go to classes. She entered learning as soon as she moved away. Attitudes to education sometimes mellow over time, and husbands, even Fathema's, have changed their attitudes, now encouraging their wives to learn. Shalina's in laws have slowly altered their attitude and now say that she can start English classes when her youngest starts school. This is, however, a few years in the future. Sofia is still confined to the house.

Domestic labour

Domestic labour, usually referred to as 'duties,' tends to take precedence over learning. Large families are common and there are often elderly relatives to care for. As we saw earlier, in-laws and husbands can force women into domestic servitude whilst others are more liberal but offer no practical support.

Women who grew up in the UK as well as those who migrated as adults often choose to stay at home when their children are young and plan to take up learning later in life. Sometimes the realities of limited time and the amount and burden of work entailed in caring for large families of up to ten children, older adults and husbands with little or no support means that women simply can't learn. Lubna, for instance, who grew up in the UK, can't see any chance of learning at present because she is so busy with her four children.

Pregnancy and the birth of children is a significant trigger in giving up English classes or hindering the ability of women to attend. Women who had been learning frequently stopped when they had their first baby. Mothers had a stop-start learning pattern where they left classes when pregnant, started again when their child was aged one or two then left during the next pregnancy. This considerably delayed their progress.

The mothers who want to learn and are encouraged by their families do not foresee starting until their children are settled in school. This is viewed as a positive choice to care for their young children and not want to put them in nurseries. However, women who then did not return to classes for over fifteen years now regret this choice. Aspia, who is in an Entry level 2 class said:

> *'I wish I had learned eighteen years ago. If I studied when I came maybe I would be fluent now'.*

Iram stays in the house where her children keep her entertained, but would also like to go to college to 'feed my passion' for art.

Other women are willing to leave their children with carers; Mariam for instance believes nurseries are good for children as, like her three year old, they can make friends and learn English. These women are often thwarted by a shortage of affordable crèche and childcare places. Women who are allowed to go to classes but have no childcare support at home often fail to find childcare. Abida, who grew up in the UK and left school after 'O' levels to work wanted to go back to studying. However, she couldn't balance studying with childcare and the distance involved in travelling to the nearest course and gave up the beauty therapy course she had started.

Health and age

Poor health, often coupled with lack of confidence, low self esteem or childcare problems prevents women going out to classes. One woman said she now has depression and lacks confidence to attend a class. Some women simply think they are not capable of learning.

One group of women not in learning describe themselves as 'too old' and 'worn out' to learn, saying education is not their priority at this stage in their lives. Women in the 'too old to learn' group span ages 44 to 71. Mrs. Ali, a 71 year old Pakistani woman did not study when she arrived in the UK 31 years ago as she had no transport and did not know her way around the area. She rues this now but says she is old and it's too late to learn. Like other 'older' women, she thinks it is too difficult to understand and learn in old age.

Women in their 40s also describe themselves as too old to learn as they are too unconfident or embarrassed to go to classes. One of these is a 44 year old Somali woman who has never been to any kind of school and says that the prospect of starting at this stage of her life is too daunting. At the same time she would like more of the independence that learning English could give her. Her timidity contrasts with other women in their forties who have strong aspirations to improve their English and go to work when their children grow up. Khadija, a Somali woman who has had a stroke is learning very slowly but says she is determined to continue as she has many problems without English and:

'Learning is better than not learning.'

A further deterrent is a belief that older women 'don't learn' in 'our culture'. As a result some women say they would feel ashamed or embarrassed to take up learning. This is not universal though, as we also talked to women aged 50 and over who are accessing learning. Additionally, learning organisations reported a new demand from women in their 60s, often stimulated by the desire to gain citizenship

Raziya had no chance to learn when she was younger because she was looking after her children and working in the family business. She would like to learn to be more independent but thinks that people would probably laugh at her, as she is too old at over 65:

'My community would also like to see me rest and enjoy my life for what is left of it. This is no age to go back into learning. They would probably think something is definitely wrong with me because all my life I have been committed to my home and family and now I am taking up learning.'

Frequently a combination of factors prevents women from learning. Mrs Miah, for example, had a young child, a second pregnancy, and no childcare so that when her local classes stopped she did too.

Lack of information

In the 1970s and early 1980s there were fewer ESOL classes and learners were often taught in their homes, usually by volunteers. Women who arrived in the 1970s had benefited from this home tuition either individually or in small groups with family and neighbours. It was the only education they had but suddenly it stopped. They didn't know why their tutor stopped coming and received no guidance about alternatives. Their learning finished at this point and they felt this prevented them from fulfilling their potential.

For years lack of information has deterred women from finding classes. Women who arrived 17 and 21 years ago did not know where to find a class and received no help or information. This had long-term consequences for those such as Khadija, aged 64, who never found out where to learn English. She got by for many years, but was miserable and frustrated that she couldn't help her children with their schoolwork. She managed, but 'sometimes, even now, I feel angry with myself for missing out on learning English.'

In reference to the current situation, women talked about lack of access to information and spending up to two years not knowing how to access a class. This is more common where women live on their own or lead an isolated life.

Fees

State funded ESOL was free to eligible learners until September 2007 when fees were introduced. Learners in receipt of means tested benefits are eligible for fee remission and there is a discretionary learner hardship fund to assist women with no independent income or who cannot provide proof of benefit. However, information about the changes has not been consistently communicated to those they affect. Not all the women have received accurate information about the new fee requirements and remissions and some have heard about the introduction of fees but do not know that they could be eligible for remission. This has deterred them from trying to join classes.

Women attending English classes said they are able to attend several classes a week because they are free, either because the organisation subsidises them or they are eligible for the discretionary Hardship Fund or fee remission. These women are worried that fees will be introduced for them from 2008 as this means they will not be able to afford to enrol for the same number of classes. They intend to try to carry on learning by enrolling for fewer hours of provision to reduce the costs, but told us that even this will depend on their husbands agreeing to pay. Learning organisations also identified rising concerns about fees because learners' husbands hold the purse strings and are often reluctant to pay fees for their wives to learn English which makes the women drop out. In contrast, one teacher said that payment has made learners value their learning and reduced drop out. Providers also regarded the requirement for newly arrived spouses and fiancées to wait a year for eligibility to access state funded provision as problematic as it excludes women with an urgent need to learn English.

Lack of accessible provision

The provision on offer is not suitable for everyone. Women who cannot access learning outside the home because of family or domestic pressures have no options, as there are very few home tuition schemes. A number of our respondents told us that shyness and nervousness stops them going out to a class. Distance, where there are no nearby classes, also constitutes a huge barrier to those unable to travel. Some women aren't permitted to mix with men outside the home in learning environments so require women only learning opportunities but often find the only classes on offer are mixed.

Long waiting lists prevent women accessing provision. We heard the frustration of women who have waited months or years for space in a class. Hinda arrived in 2001 as an asylum seeker with no English. She spent over two years on a waiting list for a course. She is now attending college four days a week but, because of wasted time, has only reached Entry three level seven years after her arrival. She feels she is now making progress and aspires to train as a nurse when her English is better to attain her childhood ambition:

'Everyone has a dream.'

Some of the Somali women had tried classes and left because they felt they were 'no good'. Their reasons were that teachers didn't make much effort, resources were poor, there was not enough speaking practice, noisy groups, mixed levels and not being able to understand the teachers.

Providers also acknowledged the attitudinal, cultural, personal, practical and structural factors identified by the women as barriers to taking part in and progressing in learning.

'Family commitments and pressures, cultural restraints/expectations, lack of confidence in functioning independently, husbands, children under 5.' (Curriculum leader)

Employment

The women's experiences of work varied. A small number worked before migrating to the UK, but failed to attain the same level of work with lack of English language as a contributory factor. About half of the women interviewed had undertaken paid employment outside the home in a variety of occupations. Others have never worked. Explanations for not working in the UK echo those for not taking up learning; personal choice, childcare, domestic duties, or active opposition from husband or family.

The occupations of the eleven Pakistani and Bangladeshi women born and brought up in the UK differ, but the pattern of giving up work when they start a family is common. Ten of them worked before they were married; in childcare, retail, administration, architecture and law. One left her job because she was being sexually harassed, the others to look after their children. Two described themselves as wealthy enough not to work.

The most common occupations of the women migrants are cleaning, factory work in textiles and food production, home sewing and retail. One woman teaches Bengali to children, and two Somali women are volunteer interpreter and community project workers. A small number of these women had worked in their home countries, with the Somali women more likely to have worked in Somalia or Europe. A pattern of settling for low paid or lower grade work than their original occupation is common across all three groups, often because of limited English language skills.

Lack of childcare, family responsibilities and attitudes towards women working as well as poor language skills are, in general, the major obstacles to employment outside the home for the women we interviewed. Husbands and in-laws, who do not permit women to learn, also do not allow them to work. However, this is changing. Yasmin, for example, commented that even five years ago there would be gossip in the Bangladeshi community in Lancashire if women worked but this is less so now. Maka said views are changing in her Somali community and more women are considering going into work and are not so 'housewife oriented'. Somali women like Leyla said the community wants to see more Somali professionals in the UK and people look up to her with respect and pride.

Support for women's employment is not without its limits. As with learning English, the view that family responsibilities must come first was reiterated, and the acceptability of working is often conditional on the children's ages and whether elders or sick relatives need care at home. Some women mentioned that the type of occupation is an important factor in its acceptability; it should be 'respectable', whilst some believe that women should not work where they have to talk to strangers or men. Women like Halimo meet this challenge by working at home taking in home sewing. Age also appears to be a factor, with employment more acceptable for younger women and women who grew up in the UK. Ferdousara, who grew up in the UK, and her husband both work part time and share the housework. In contrast, new brides are often not allowed to work outside the home and have to do all the domestic labour. The teenage women interviewed in this study all assume that they will work before they get married and carry on after they have children.

The women referred to the importance of role models, with some acting as a role model themselves. Rekha, a young Bengali woman who grew up in the UK who has a BA in Architecture has found that gender discrimination and prejudice against her wearing a headscarf make it difficult to secure work. In the past she worked voluntarily in architecture firms to demonstrate to people in her community that women can have a challenging career. She said that she has influenced other women to go into architecture and been an inspiration to some of her peers; her community are supportive and proud of her.

Most of the women aspire to paid employment at some point in the future. They are motivated for a number of reasons; they want a wage to contribute to the family income, to improve their standard of living and to buy luxuries for their children. Claimants do not want to subsist on benefits. They want to build careers to be proud of and act as role models for others. Enriching their own lives is highly important; working will help them feel proud, keep busy, do something for themselves, feel happier and healthier, be more independent and alert, and boost their confidence and self-esteem. Sirad, for example said she was more confident when she was working and would like to work part time to boost her self-esteem, and Deeba wants to work to 'keep my mind fresh.'

Wakaran needs to work to pay off the debts and bills following her husband's death. Not only is she hampered by her lack of English, she fears she will have difficulty finding childcare. Moreover she worries that she will lose her children to her in-laws as they are trying to gain custody, saying she is not a fit mother. The neighbours support her and will help with the childcare. She feels torn because she does not want to leave her children with carers and has always 'been there for them' but needs to find a job to 'make ends meet'.

Language becomes a factor when we look at plans and aspirations. Some of the women identified their lack of English as a barrier to working and a need to learn English before looking for a job. Others view work as an environment where they can improve their English, observing that they pick up some English at work. For Halima, poor English not only restricts the type of job she can do, but prevents her travelling far to work. English is not required for low paid occupations such as cleaning and some women chose them for this reason. Others who have worked in local shops or factories employing other women from their community observed they were happy and comfortable there. Two speculated that maybe they would have got more English customers if they had spoken English whilst some women said the barrier to working isn't language but going outside the home to work.

Community

We asked women about the types of communities they live in, their relationships with others in their community, community activity and their views of their communities. The majority of the women interviewed live in communities where most other people are from a similar background. A smaller number live in neighbourhoods where residents are from different backgrounds and ethnic groups and one or two live in predominantly white areas.

With few exceptions, the women who live in communities where most of the other residents are from a similar ethnic and cultural background choose to live there and feel very positive about their lives in these communities. They prefer to live near others from their culture and background with all the amenities they need, such as shops selling Halal food, mosques and schools. This does not mean that they want to be segregated from other people and communities. Women living in mixed or predominantly white areas have more mixed views. Some enjoy quiet, affluent areas and others the vibrancy and diversity of cosmopolitan environments. Those living in poorer estates often encounter problems from racist neighbours or drugs and crime in the neighbourhood.

Leyla's story

"Without any type of education you are nothing"

Leyla (41) came to the UK 14 years ago as a refugee from Somalia and now lives in Tower Hamlets, London with her husband and four children. Leyla had the chance to study Psychology and Arabic at Cairo University and in Somalia ran her own business and worked at the Algerian Embassy as secretary to the Ambassador.

She says her Somali community are positive about women working and helping their community.

In spite of her prior education and work experience, Leyla didn't think she could learn English. But in the UK she has undertaken a number of courses – learning English for four years up to Level 3, and achieving Level 3 NVQ in IT and GCSE Mathematics. Learning English has transformed her life. On a personal level, her confidence has improved. It has also positively impacted upon her family and community. She works as an interpreter and translator for other Somalis, assists with letter writing and form filling and helps run a local Somali women's group. She is very involved with her children's education, helping them with their homework, talking to their schoolteachers and helping run the Homework Club in their school.

Leyla has a passion for learning and has undertaken courses to help her set up and run her own business and would like to learn bookkeeping and perhaps accounting. Her present priority is to get a job and perhaps fit studying around that. She says she is ambitious and having worked in Somalia and in a voluntary capacity in the UK, wants to build her career and, along with her husband, provide financial security for her family.

She has a strong sense of community and has a number of Somali and Bengali friends. She found that being able to communicate in English has made a big difference especially in making friends with new people from different backgrounds. But most of all she is happy where she lives and feels confident about her position in her community.

Values, belonging and support

Almost all the women living in predominantly Asian or Somali communities, whether immigrants or brought up in the UK, value the sense of belonging in tight knit communities that are 'like a big family.' They prize the high levels of support available, feel solidarity with people close by and can call on them for assistance. Rukhsana, a bilingual woman, does not want to move away because she appreciates the common values and neighbourhood unity. Neela would find it impossible to live anywhere else:

'I would never move very far from my community because I fit in very well in my neighbourhood and also the community. I love my neighbours like I do my family and would find it very hard to move away from my community'.

Fitting in is important. Amina, who wears a full Burka, feels comfortable in her Muslim area but would feel awkward in a non-Muslim community. On the other hand, a small minority of the women find the closeness and cultural uniformity stifling. Sabeen goes to the mosque but also to the cinema and discos and doesn't cover her head. She wants to move away as she feels different and judged. Others said that their community is too gossipy and censorious and they have no privacy, as everyone knows everyone else's business. Tasneem, for example, feels trapped in her house because is worried about gossip and judgement if she goes out on her own:

'Thinking about others stops me doing a lot of things like I won't even go out on my own even local shopping because people may talk and say things like what is she doing outside on her own without her kids or husband.'

Most women feel a strong sense of solidarity with others in the predominantly Asian or Somali areas. They value having family nearby and opportunities to socialise with family and friends. They emphasise that it is Asian culture to be a good neighbour. Helping each other, whether to provide another pair of hands for family celebrations, or during periods of sickness or trouble or shop for elders is also valued.

Other women in the community are a source of support for women such as Sofia who are oppressed by their husbands; for example they try to mediate to convince her family to loosen the constraints on learning English. Some women are isolated and stay in the house all the time because of a lack of English and/or other factors such as in-laws or husbands keeping them in, lack of confidence, ill health or depression.

Many of the women who are happy in their community like the fact they can communicate in 'their own language.' This is particularly important for the women with little English. The younger women, who have grown up bilingual in the UK such as Lubna, can be the only fluent English speaker in a mixed area. She is frequently called on to translate or make telephone calls. Even where women are pleased to help, it can become a burden and Lubna prefers the area she has moved to where her friends are other Asian mothers who are fluent in English.

Community communications

Relationships with neighbours in white or mixed communities ranged from friendly, through indifferent to hostile or racist. A number of women have friendships that span different cultures and religions and enjoy socialising and visiting with neighbours. Some Somali women, for example, enjoy living in an area of Liverpool they describe as 'cosmopolitan'. They mix with other mothers, use the libraries and take their children to after school clubs and sports centres. Several women told us they rarely socialise with others in their area.

One reason is they gave is that lots of poor families in their communities won't speak to them or are threatening or racist. Feeling safe is very important. The women want to feel safe and free from harassment in their community and this is achieved by knowing the other people. They say that Asian and Somali areas are safe whereas mixed areas are often seen as threatening or dangerous. Khadija is 'scared' of going to live in a remote place. Women in mixed areas, which they describe as 'rough', are subjected to racism and sometimes nuisance and harassment from local children and youths. Some of these areas are rife with crime, drugs and people on benefit 'hanging around all day'. Fear of 'drugs people' makes some women scared to walk around outside. Others prefer to keep themselves apart. Even where they do not feel in immediate danger, they are hesitant to interact with their neighbours in case they are hassled or harassed.

Other women have 'polite' or cordial relationships with neighbours in which they largely keep themselves to themselves because they have limited time for interaction, personal preference, they are shy or they can't speak English. English language is one of the factors that influence interaction and socialising with people outside the women's own ethnic groups. Some of the women learning English said it had given them the confidence to chat to their neighbours and some now visit each other's houses. They said they are 'more comfortable,' and 'It feels terrible if you can't talk.' Women with little proficiency in English are, understandably, often reluctant to try to converse in English because of their skills, and say lack of English prevents them making friends. Some greet their neighbours but can't have a conversation. Mrs Ali, for example, always says 'hello' to her neighbours as she regards this as a common courtesy but can't say anything else.

English is not the only factor however, and confidence level often combines with English to influence interactions with English speakers. Women such as Mrs Begum said they are too shy and unconfident to try to speak. She enjoys socialising and being able to communicate, but having a laugh with neighbours and friends is missing in her life because of her low confidence. Anwara says the English women at her children's school are friendly but she feels she can't chat so says 'hello' then walks away. In contrast, women like Shalina and Nimo, have similar levels of English but more confidence try to communicate whenever they have an opportunity.

Community engagement

There is a high level of informal involvement in community activities, but relatively low levels of formal community participation. This mirrors the lack of take up of learning and work. As with participation in learning and work, caring responsibilities and domestic duties affect the extent to which women are active in their communities. Personal inclination, shyness and confidence also play a part. English is one of a number of obstacles preventing women from interacting with neighbours and community participation.

Community activity is more likely to be informal activity with a women's own ethnic or religious community. Most women are involved in informal activity and groups in their own communities. This relates to the value placed on good neighbouring outlined above and takes the form of socialising, shopping for sick people or elders and helping at family or community functions. One woman, for example, organises charity fundraising in her community. The Somali women are especially likely to be active in community activities at the mosque and Somali cultural events. There are strong women's groups offering support and activities for these women.

There is little take up of organised opportunities, such as community events, tenants groups or Sure Start Children's Centre sessions outside their own cultural groups, although the bilingual women who grew up in the UK tend to be more active in their communities. Some of the women in learning also regularly attend community events and see them as an important part of their lives. A few women have attended Sure Start Children's Centre sessions but their experiences have been mixed. Some met other mothers and learned a lot whereas others found the experience alien or the people unwelcoming.

Reasons given by those who don't take up community services or take part in group or events are lack of time, caring for in laws, poor health or poor English. Some report lack of information or encouragement from services and groups. Shyness and low confidence is a significant factor. Sultana, a Bangladeshi woman, was encouraged by her husband to attend baby groups. However, she has never been as she thinks she will struggle with the language. Tasneem, a Bangladeshi woman describes herself as 'not a confident person' who prefers being at home with her family. She would not 'feel right' getting involved in social groups and would feel she didn't belong if English was the main language.

There are a few instances of women organising groups or doing voluntary work but, as in the general population, this activity is not widespread. Some women were not interested or said women in their community do not do voluntary work. Others said they are interested and explained their lack of current activity in terms of shortage of time, low confidence or poor English. Shanaz was born in the UK but said she lacks confidence to get involved in the wider community. She sees this as an individual trait rather than one connected to culture or learning. Women like Wakaran and Shaheen plan to take up community activity later in their lives when they have learned English or their children are older. The women who undertake voluntary work are, on the whole, more confident and have higher levels of fluency in English. Shajida, who is a parent governor and undertakes voluntary youth work and runs a women's drug awareness group, grew up in the UK, and Leyla who is very active running local Somali groups and a homework club at her children's school, is a graduate and has level 3 English as well as 'an active disposition' and confident personality.

Summary

Interviews with the women revealed the diversity and complexities of their educational experiences, lives, identities and relationships with their families and communities. We found inconsistencies and contradictions as well as common trends in attitudes to women's learning amongst the women, their families and communities, and learned that views are changing so that appreciation of the importance of women's learning is becoming more widespread.

The women all value English language. Those with few English skills are painfully aware of the limitations this places on their lives and almost all want to learn. They identified the factors that hinder their learning; poor prior or no learning experiences, the expectations of their families and husbands, restrictions that husbands and in laws place on their lives, the demands of caring responsibilities and domestic labour, poor health, age, low confidence, financial constraints and structural barriers that include lack of information, lack of local, accessible classes and lack of appropriate and affordable childcare.

Experiences of paid employment and community engagement are similarly very diverse. Women who work are often employed in occupations which do not require proficiency in English. The women we interviewed, on the whole, live in predominantly Asian or Somali communities where they value features such as solidarity and support, safety, shared values and neighbourhood unity. English language is an important influence on participation in English speaking workplaces and English speaking communities. Language skills can combine with the factors identified above as limiting participation in learning to affect employment opportunities and community involvement. Additionally, external factors such as safety, racism and the attitudes of employers, residents and community based services and groups affect levels of paid employment and community activity.

The women's stories demonstrate that English is not the only factor affecting achievement of their dreams and their family, work and community lives. At the same we can see that English language is undoubtedly an important condition for greater freedom, independence and choice in these areas. We will now examine the factors that have enabled Bangladeshi, Pakistani and Somali women to access and advance in English language learning.

5. Women in learning

The previous section gave us a glimpse into the lives of Bangladeshi, Pakistani and Somali women, their aspirations, views on and barriers to accessing learning. In this section we examine how the women not in organised learning suggest removing limitations to participation in learning, what enables the women who access English classes to do so and what learning organisations such as colleges, adult education services and voluntary sector organisations do to reach and support these women to achieve.

We interviewed 38 Bangladeshi, Pakistani and Somali women attending ESOL provision in adult education, further education or voluntary sector organisations in different towns and cities. Their ages range from 16 to women in their 60s and their levels from Entry level 2 to levels 1 and 2. They include young unmarried women, married women and widows, and women with and without children. Most have attended classes for over two years and have progressed from a starting point of being able to use very little English. Although their motivations and aspirations differ, they share a determination to continue learning to help them realise their ambitions. Their testimonies yield interesting insights into the approaches and support that enable them to access and persist in learning.

As noted in the context section, the evidence indicates that a substantial majority of providers take little specific action to attract these groups of women into learning. In some places provision to attract them is diminishing in the face of competition for places from other groups of learners and the diminution of funding for lower levels. We do recognise, however, that this is by no means universal; some providers do continue to work with these groups and others are starting to turn their attention to them. This section portrays approaches adopted by tutors and managers from statutory and voluntary sector organisations who are making active efforts to offer learning to Bangladeshi, Pakistani or Somali women. Some of these organisations carry out work in local communities to attract women, but not exclusively Bangladeshi, Pakistani and Somali women whilst others target this group, sometimes seeking to work with the most excluded women within these groups, for instance, women with mental health problems. A few enrol women from these groups when they turn up, but do not actively seek to recruit them.

We gathered provider perspectives through an online survey, telephone interviews and visits to a range of providers spread across the country. We visited three Further Education colleges, one Adult Education Service and one Voluntary and Community sector organisation. We carried out ten telephone interviews with two colleges, two training providers, two voluntary and community sector organisations and five adult learning services. Eleven learning providers completed the online questionnaire in full; five respondents were managers or tutors employed in Further Education, four in Adult and Community Learning and the other two were a charity and a women's group.

The learning they provide is mostly discrete ESOL at different levels in college or community settings. In addition, a number of subjects with embedded language are offered, such as craft, sewing, childcare, health and social care, gardening and arts. Some colleges have embedded ESOL or literacy into vocational courses such as Science or Health and Beauty. Family learning is an important way of reaching women whilst English for citizenship is in demand in some areas but not in others. A small number of providers focus on entry to employment and offer assistance with training and accessing employment. Some have a policy of employing women from Pakistani, Bangladeshi and Somali communities to work locally as tutors, learner support assistants, administration staff and centre managers. One provider stressed the importance of planning at local authority level to ensure provision meets local needs, but most planning took place in individual organisations.

Learner cohorts

A strong message which emerged from the provider interviews is that, as other work has shown (see for example Baynham *et al*. 2007, Dalziel and Sofres 2005, Roberts *et al*. 2004), the learner cohorts can be very diverse. Ages vary and at least two of the providers note that the learner profile has recently started to change as women aged 50 plus who have been in the country for 30 to 40 years have started to access English classes as they want to apply for citizenship. This means that groups are often mixed. They might include women aged 18 to over 65 and women who have been in the country for some time alongside recent arrivals. A large proportion of the women in community provision are pre entry or Entry levels 1 and 2.

Over the last few years there has been a change in the learner profile in some areas. Younger women with higher levels of qualifications from their own country, and some English skills are joining classes to generally improve their English, especially their speaking and listening. The level of education in their own country gives an indication of their English skills. There is a perception that community classes are for lower level learners only. The higher the level, the less likely they are to attend community provision; they go to college.

One provider in the North of England observed some general differences between Pakistani and Bangladeshi learners in their town, characterising the Bangladeshi women as usually at a lower level than Pakistani learners. Another identified different characteristics of learners, typifying Pakistani women as outgoing and more likely to attend groups, Bangladeshi women as quieter and more reluctant to join mixed groups and Somali women as 'upfront and open'. Provision is thus organised to meet different expectations and comfort zones. This observation cannot be generalised to all women in these groups, but it does remind us that to treat Pakistani, Bangladeshi and Somali women as a homogeneous group can conceal the differential situations and learning needs that our research reveals.

Breaking the barriers

Our interviews demonstrate that it is easier for some women to access learning than others, and they indicate that providers are succeeding in connecting with more of these 'easier to reach' women. There appears to be a greater thirst for learning in some communities and in these areas, organisers reflect that it is easier to attract women into learning than in the past when they had to do a lot of 'door knocking'. Women learning told us they experienced little family opposition as long as they prioritised family.

When asked what makes learning accessible the two most frequent answers were childcare provision and local learning with classes timed to fit in with school hours, for both English and other subjects. We heard from learners who are enabled to study by the availability of nursery places, for children as young as six months in one community learning centre. This was the exception however, and we frequently heard of shortages of crèche places, restrictions on the age of children that can be cared for and recent cuts to crèche provision. Some providers are unable to provide any childcare because no funding has been allocated.

Information and encouragement from friends, family and community members and trusted agencies such as schools are highly effective ways of getting women to classes. In addition, outreach support to overcome women's lack of confidence to get to a class, women only classes, bilingual tutors, and support in the class are important accessibility strategies. The learning organisations we spoke to mostly suggested similar strategies and told us about their approaches to recruitment, retention and progression.

Spreading the word

Numerous methods are employed to recruit women to programmes. Community outreach emerged as the most used and the most effective. Other strategies include working in partnership and liaising with relevant people in the community; asking learners to spread the word, using national events such as International Women's Week to promote provision, taster sessions, summer schools, offering support for learners and accessible admissions processes.

Virtually none of the women we spoke to had found classes through written publicity or by approaching a learning organisation. The most common way of finding classes is informally through recommendation and word of mouth from relatives, friends, neighbours, students and others in the community. Providers recognise this and, like learners, consider personal recommendation and word of mouth as one of the most effective recruitment methods. .

Targeted outreach might involve employing Community Learning Co-ordinators, outreach workers, voluntary or paid learning champions or a community engagement team, often using bilingual workers where practical. Outreach workers in the community reach women through the places they go to in the course of their everyday lives, especially schools, nurseries, doctors' surgeries and baby clinics, places of worship, factories and community groups. Learning champions use their expertise and contacts, and women who are already learners inform and encourage others. Visiting women in their homes is used as a strategy although this is less common.

These approaches are not quite so effective where women do not live near others from their ethnic group or in areas where there are no networks to connect with. One adult education service said they have found no evidence that there is a communication network within the community they serve, and information isn't spread by word of mouth as it is in a nearby town. Recruitment strategies take this into account.

Learners and providers identified local organisations, especially voluntary organisations; asylum seeker and refugee support organisations, schools, nurseries and Sure Start Children's Centres plus key workers such as library staff, health visitors and social workers as important sources of information and referral. Ghazala failed to find classes in Manchester but was helped by a Sure Start worker when she moved to Liverpool. Jobcentre plus was only once identified as a source of referral, perhaps because most of the women are not seeking employment:

Community learning providers stress the benefits of building reputation and trust. One project, established for over ten years, said that people approach the centre as they know it is a tried, trusted and friendly place which is sensitive to their needs and employs bilingual staff. Open days, coffee sessions, social events and taster courses can provide an informal and enjoyable first taste of learning. They enable women to voice their interests and needs in a welcoming and safe environment and allow them to try and enjoy activities that could inspire them to take up further learning:

'At these events we organise food, fashion shows, and henna painting to draw people in. This has been a proven method and has worked really well.'

When asked why these approaches work, learning organisers say it is because they are personal, and different languages can be used for verbal communication. As some of the women are not literate in either English or their mother tongue, this is the most appropriate way to reach them. As one tutor suggested, being non-confrontational, reliable, warm and friendly is the best approach to take:

"Meeting with the women works well with those who might not be able to read any literature about classes. Their questions can be answered thus helping overcome any barriers they may have and also gaining their trust. Publicity in different languages also attracts well, especially those who are literate" (Tutor).

Making learning accessible

Making sure that women know where to access provision and stimulating their interest is essential to start them on their learning journey. Strategies are then needed to address any attitudinal and practical barriers to ensure that access to learning is straightforward and women are supported to stay with their courses long enough to make headway in their learning.

Practical ways of supporting women learners include financial help such as free provision or reduced fees; high quality, affordable crèche provision; holding classes in accessible locations; sensitive timetabling; content tailored to groups; and a supportive, friendly atmosphere. More attitudinal or emotional forms of support include ensuring that the attitude of tutors is one that helps instil confidence in the women, that tutors keep in contact with the women, and that they recognise and celebrate their learning. All are important in motivating and enabling women to stay the course.

Location

The location of learning can determine whether women are able to access learning. Those unable to attend classes because of their husband's or family opposition, caring responsibilities or ill health suggested individual or group home tuition as a solution:

'Its better if a teacher comes to my home then I can look after daughter and learn English'

Travel is a barrier for women where learning sites are some distance from their homes. Some colleges that only offer a main site location do offer assistance with travel information and costs. However, this is conditional on funding, and one college that used to offer travel cards said funding was no longer available.

A more widespread approach is to offer learning in local settings. Schools, community centres, churches, mosques, nurseries and childcare centres are typical venues. The importance of 'safe' environments was stressed time and again. Reluctant husbands were more likely to allow their wives to attend family learning in a safe school environment to help their children, and from there many women progress to community provision:

"Offering classes in places/venues where they are comfortable and within the vicinity of their homes" (Curriculum Leader).

A women's centre that offers learning is an ideal venue as it is accessible and easy to reach for women in the community in which it is located. A women only environment can provide a sense of security and attract women who might not go to a mixed centre. The appeal of the centre is heightened if it is welcoming and has space to relax and socialise. Learning can be informal but purposeful.

Women-only provision

It is impossible for some women to attend mixed classes for religious or cultural reasons. We saw in the previous section the suspicion and lack of trust some women face at home. Women-only classes are one solution to this. Some of the women who are not restricted by their family also said they tend to feel more comfortable in women-only groups. This environment helps them to make progress, as they are not shy, can talk 'women's secrets' and ask the teacher advice. Although some of these women would be able to continue learning if mixed classes were the only option, they said they would feel inhibited from speaking in class.

A 'girls' college' aimed specifically at 16-18 year olds in Stoke-on-Trent has recently been established for girls who would have otherwise just left school. It offers Business Administration and Childcare courses and in the first year (2007/08) staff have been focusing on girls who are likely to leave school and stay at home. This women-only college is in the middle of the local community and is a 'safe environment'. Staff are currently working hard to build up trust with parents through personal contact with the parents and an open day to inform the community.

Fadumo's story

Fadumo is a strict Muslim and a single parent who is quite isolated. She wanted to learn in a women-only group and to engage in formal learning. In 2006 she started with 3 Entry 1 ESOL women-only classes and achieved a certificate. During the year the women's class joined lots of recreational and craft activities but Fadumo never engaged with this and remained quite isolated. However, she brought her son into the summer family learning classes, which were an outreach programme from the central library. As a result she began using her local library. In 2007-08 the ESOL women's class funding ran out and as it closed Fadumo was signposted to either Employability or Patchwork. The Patchwork group was the only women-only group in the centre so she opted for this although it was not her interest. Initially she didn't engage in the sewing activities and left the class as soon as it was over. She didn't appear to value the sewing as much as the formal English. During the first term she began to sew at home and to bring it back to show other women, and as a result began to make friends with the other women on the course. She now has her own social networks and has also moved up another level in her ESOL learning.

Meeting need

Learning provider staff stress the importance of offering flexible provision to cater for need. At the same time they report closure of this sort of provision as a result of funding cuts and pressure to achieve targets. One was able to open classes in response to demand in the past, but this year the funding has been capped, resulting in waiting lists, whilst another provider noted that a lot of their community classes have recently closed because of cuts in funding.

Some expressed a strong view that more money and investment is required, especially for beginners who need pre-entry programmes. Several talked about caps or cuts in provision and waiting lists. There is concern that funding cuts and targets are threatening Entry level 1 and 2 provision, which will impact on these learners disproportionately.

Flexible provision at convenient times is important as is a 'roll on roll off model' which enables women to join at any time and doesn't restrict them to September enrolment:

> *"They can select the time most suitable. Many are allowed to attend 15 mins late or leave early to drop off/pick up children" (ESOL Lecturer).*

Providers have started to introduce attendance rules to help achieve targets or as a mechanism for rationing provision in the face of huge demand. These stricter rules mean that irregular attendees or those who disappear for a period then want to return risk losing their places to learners who attend well and are given enrolment priority.

One view is that women attend more regularly and are less likely to drop out as a result. Others hold this position in general but are sensitive to the risk factors and have introduced strategies to mitigate the impact. Holidays are times when learners are at risk of dropping out as they get out of the habit of attending class so some tutors contact their learners to remind them to return. One has an 'amnesty' system so that women can take extended leave to travel to Pakistan or Bangladesh for holidays, family illness or bereavement. Some providers do not count missing a class as an absence if the student informs them in advance. A refugee support project agrees absences due to childcare issues, noting that this can contrast with more strict policies at some colleges where learners lose their place if they miss three classes. This project also has an 'open door' policy where women can return after sickness absence.

One teacher noticed that Bangladeshi women are particularly shy when learning with women from other backgrounds and are reluctant to learn anywhere other than in Bangladeshi community centres. In response, they organise specific Bangladeshi courses made up of 90 per cent Bangladeshi women which they say has very good results.

Recreational activities such as women only swimming trips, visits to a health suite, yoga tasters, sewing, crafts with henna, country walks, visits to the library and family learning are popular with women from this group. Many of the above events have been funded through the Home Office. Though this funding has ceased, the voluntary organisation offering this programme continues to look for alternative funding. It also offers informal activities such as lunches where learners can bring food to share which doesn't require extra funding. This approach attracts women to join and stay in English language courses.

In Section 4 we saw that almost all the women not currently in organised learning do want to take it up at some stage, either now or in the future, and usually when their youngest children reach school age. With the obvious exception of the women for whom English is a first language, developing English is a common priority. It should be noted that it is seen as a means to achieve the wide range of aspirations described in the previous section. A wide range of other vocational, personal, community development and creative subjects also appeal. Vocational interests include information technology, beauty therapy, health and social care, childcare and classroom assistant qualifications as well as nursing, teaching and business. Driving was frequently mentioned as a passport to achieving greater mobility and independence. Other women wish to develop their artistic talent through henna painting, painting and drawing. Acquiring skills to develop initiatives to help other women in their communities was also mentioned, whilst Islamic school is the priority for one of the Somali women.

Staying the course

Strategies to help women learners stay the course and create the conditions in which they can make progress, often in the face of competing pressures from home and family, are predominantly those relating to the quality of the teaching and learning. Providers said that the recognised quality elements that are appropriate for all learners, including excellent teaching, and appropriate assessment and tutorial support, must be in place. When combined with specific inclusion strategies, they can be mutually reinforcing in the interests of the more excluded learners such as the women in this study. They are effective mainly because they are relevant, they are targeted, they help to develop trust between tutors and learners and help learners achieve their goals.

No one approach emerged as a solution adopted by all the learning providers responding to the online survey and interviews. Different strategies were put forward which related to the planning and delivery of teaching and learning, staffing, assessment, timetabling and other forms of support.

Of these, content that relates to life experiences and interests, praise and encouragement, recognising success, class dynamics and social outings, understanding tutors and advice regarding progression and tutorials and learner representation emerged as the most successful strategies. Social contact, a variety of activities, crèche provision, tutorials and qualifications were all deemed effective. In the case of social contact it was noted that attending learning might be the only opportunity some women have to socialise. It is a good chance to make new friends whilst praise and encouragement are important for women with low self-esteem and helps to build their confidence.

Quality teaching

Learners and providers concurred in the view that tutors are key to learners persevering and achieving. We heard from learners who stopped classes because they did not rate the tutors and teaching. Conversely, those who did stay attribute this to their teachers and their positive learning experiences. In essence, tutors' attitudes are as important as their language teaching skills. Learners value teachers who can build their trust, who understand their lives, raise their confidence and make learning interesting by relating the content to their concerns and interests. Teachers who encourage and praise them, recognise and celebrate their achievements, and find ways to extend the learning beyond the walls of the classroom are appreciated.

It is clear that the relationship the tutors have with their learners is significant, and that good relationships with tutors and peers encourage learners to attend and keep learning. It is crucial, therefore, that teachers foster positive classroom dynamics, starting, as one provider notes, with proactive efforts to welcome and manage the integration of new learners into classes. Learners' value social relationships and can continue learning because of friendships they make in classes.

One provider noted that teachers with a good reputation attract learners as word spreads. This can be built through a stable workforce with little turnover. This is challenging for some managers who said they find it very difficult to attract good quality teachers who have the right interpersonal skills especially for the lower level learners. A further teacher quality is training and experience in working with learners at pre-entry/entry 1 as many women learners from these groups have little or no educational experience and little or no literacy in any language. This experience helps ensure that their learning needs are understood and addressed.

Respondents find that teacher training does not automatically equip teachers for working with these groups of women. One emphasised that in addition to language teaching skills, teachers need to be culturally sensitive and aware of factors that might affect learning. For her, the Level 4 teaching qualification[18] is no indication that a tutor has the right skills for the job. Often their experience, understanding and attitudes are as important, but providers are unable to employ them if they do not have the Level 4 qualification.

Responsive curriculum

Learners and teachers said that the content of classes must be tailored to learners' needs and reflect their interests which are very diverse:

> *Lots of interest in their lives and teaching scenarios that are relevant to the individual"*
>
> *(ESOL Co-ordinator).*

Since the language requirement for gaining citizenship[19] was introduced in 2002, ESOL for citizenship has been in demand. The general trend is to embed the citizenship curriculum in other courses. Teachers have found that this is a good way to give learners access to local services, opportunities and enrichment activities such as outings to museums.

In addition to life in England, learners also want to learn about and debate topical questions relating to politics and the world around them. Women want to talk about their roles and jobs and engage in interesting discussions that highlight the complexities of their different cultural experiences. They enjoy discussing issues such as history, global politics, the news, fair trade, and relationships. Others are keen on reading poems and novels. Religious topics are of interest, for example, debating human laws in contrast with 'god's laws' and ideas shared within different religions such as the concept of angels.

Learners describe some teachers and the content of classes as 'boring,' saying this makes learning more difficult: This can lead to drop out, as in the case of the learners who stopped learning because their teachers were 'no good.' One of the curriculum managers also described her struggle with teachers who resist introducing global topics, deciding on behalf of the learners that they will not be interested, even though learners in the college who do use the materials are extremely positive about them.

Provider's stress that getting the starting level right, placing women in the right class and making sure that learners' needs are met is key to keeping them in provision and supporting them to learn:

> *They help the learner to achieve their personal goals, thereby increasing motivation and allowing them to become independent"*
>
> *(Curriculum Leader).*

Several learners emphasised the need to minimise bureaucracy, stressing how off putting it can be. Some providers recognise this so ensure that assessment and Individual Learning Plan processes are very learner centred. Tutors in one organisation carry out initial assessment at the start of term then after the main

---

18. In September 2007 new qualification requirements for teaching and supporting learning in the lifelong learning sector were launched and a new 'Qualified Teacher Learning and Skills' (QTLS) status was introduced. Those undertaking a teaching role need a minimum level 4 qualification. See the LLUK website for more information http://www.lluk.org/

19. Applicants for UK settlement and citizenship must take the citizenship test or, for those below Entry Level 3, successfully complete an ESOl with citizenship course that uses approved learning materials.

enrolment date one member of staff does all the initial assessment in a community library and refers learners to the appropriate class at the right level. This provider has no mixed ability classes. Having a dedicated tutor for this has been an advantage as one point of contact with all the rules and regulations has presented the service in a professional light whilst making the process accessible.

Listening, and responding to learners' views is important. One provider carries out student surveys each term to make sure that learners' views are captured, and the information is used for their self-assessment report. Individual Learning Plans are reviewed every six weeks and again learners' comments are acted upon. Another stresses that a one to one approach through tutorials, time with the learner and on-site support works for all learners.

Supporting learners and developing their confidence

Support in the classroom helps shy learners who are lacking in confidence to stick with their course and make progress in developing their language skills. This can be nurtured through teaching and learning content and the support workers or volunteers:

> *"Lots of praise and on-going support within the group" (ESOL Co-ordinator).*

Women in the Preston group described how speaking in class has helped them to overcome their shyness and built their confidence. With the support of their tutor and peers, they have become used to speaking in front of others.

Classroom assistance is offered in different ways; learner support workers assist and encourage learners in class whilst volunteers offer one to one help and support for those learners who take more time within the group and learners are encouraged to support each other through buddy schemes. This is not without problems as funding is not always available to employ classroom support workers and one provider highlighted the absence of a consistent policy about the use of volunteers in their organisation. Lack of budget for Criminal Records Bureau (CRB) checks was also cited as a limiting factor restricting the use of volunteers and trainee teachers.

Strength of provision is the mutual support developed between learners, as well as from staff. The refugee support project, for example, encourages a peer buddying system to provide mutual support. Having bi-lingual staff can support learners with some health issues. Other providers support social networks through holding ten-minute breaks at the same time for all classes so that learners can meet with friends or women from other classes or with tutors for informal or personal discussion:

> *'It's very important that we help each other' (Rushnara).*

> *"It may be the only opportunity women get to socialise if they are expected to take responsibility for work in the home. And for women who have never previously attended school, or had their schooling interrupted by civil war or similar, the idea of qualifications is very attractive"*
>
> *(Lecturer in EAL).*

Staff and student role models are effective. The Stoke-on-Trent girls' programmes cited above are successful in part because they employ passionate women from the Asian community who become role models for learners. Some of the women referred to an informal role model system operating in one college where learners can see what others have achieved. Other colleges formalise this support; one provider often invites speakers into the courses to speak in the women's 'home' language. These speakers act as role models demonstrating how it is possible to be a housewife, have a job, be a mother and get an education.

Negative experiences of course can have the reverse effect. Zarina said that her friends say they will never go into learning following her negative experiences.

Using English outside the classroom

All the women we spoke to stressed that speaking English helps them to learn. A few women not in organised learning have tried to develop their skills by speaking with family, usually with little success. In contrast, the learning women find that using English outside the classroom reinforces their learning and is a major factor in their progress. These women are active learners, doing homework, watching television and the news in English, reading newspapers and books, visiting the library, using the Internet and talking to English people.

The women we spoke to at Preston College use the Internet to help them complete their homework and to work on their language skills. The teacher has run a short course and encouraged them to use computers at home. In the other groups, women are less likely to use computers because they don't have the skills. Others said that they don't have the time or their children monopolise the family computer.

The young women at Liverpool Community College speak English at home and with their friends and peers who are from many different nationalities. Hani, a 17-year-old unaccompanied asylum seeker, lives in a flat with people from other countries who use English as their common language. She has learnt quickly in order to survive on her own. Opportunities for the older women to speak English are more limited. Zainab, an asylum seeker, benefits from a befriending scheme organised by a refugee support project. She meets an English woman every week to talk and says they have now become friends as well as the meeting helping her improve her English. Hinda prefers to go about without an interpreter which makes her use English in real situations.

Recognising achievement

Learners said it is important to recognise what they have achieved. They said they know they have improved and what they still need to learn and they like this to be acknowledged by providers. Encouragement and celebration of achievement is important. Preston College has nominated students for the college student of the year award and taken them to a writing day at Lancaster College, for example.

More formal recognition of achievement was also valued and exams motivate some students. Younger and older learners mentioned exams as motivating, saying that they are happy when they pass. The Preston College learners are enthusiastic about exams. They view them as a milestone towards entry onto a vocational course or proof of achievement, showing that they have done something. For some, it is important 'just to be proud':

> *'We have done something and here is the proof.' (Raja).*

> *'When I go home I tell them I have learned something. It feels fantastic.' (Jahan).*

Moving on

Women in learning all have aspirations to study further or to work. Most of their learning experiences to date have been successful and positive due to a combination of personal drive and determination and, for some, sheer grit to enable them to overcome adverse external circumstances. These factors have been coupled with learning focused on their needs and with effective support from tutors. Appropriate Information, Advice and Guidance and accessible progression pathways have also made a huge difference to their learning experiences.

Aspirations

All the women in learning intend to work or to progress to vocational training once their course is completed. The four teenage learners are keen, enthusiastic and making fast progress. They attend college every day and study subjects such as IT and science as well as English. They all hope to attend university and are considering subjects such as business and nursing and they 'know where they are going'.

It is common for women to intend to train for traditional female occupations, usually, beauty, childcare and health and social care. Others aspire to higher education and professional careers such as midwifery and teaching. Although home circumstances and attitudes affect aspirations, they also appear to be influenced by their learning situations. Women attending voluntary sector provision which offers industrial sewing and childcare NVQs are seeking work in these occupations. In contrast, it is noticeable that women aim higher where they are exposed to information and encouragement to consider a wide range of options.

Progression

Providers stress the importance of good progression routes, within ESOL then onwards at the right time. Those ensure that people are referred to the most appropriate course for them and that they can move people on effectively when they are ready. At one of the organisations, tutors undertake a six weekly and termly review and can transfer learners to a more appropriate group. They often want to move together in groups, which could hold some women back, but it is explained to them that they can come to provision together, learn in different classes and meet for coffee.

A number of the colleges have improved interdepartmental communication in order to help learners to progress, for instance by offering bridging courses such as ESOL for Work, or progression pathways in specific vocational areas including Health and Social Care, Childcare and Retail. Others offer a range of courses that can include sewing, bag making and beauty. One local authority provider is trying to encourage broader learning and offer celebration events, trips and enrichment activities to help women progress onto other learning.

Information, Advice and Guidance

Information, advice and guidance are vital to provide space for women to explore their options and stepping-stones onto the next phase of their journeys. However, some teachers identify lack of funding to provide one to one support and effective guidance on progression as a problem.

We heard of approaches where the class teacher regularly discusses future options with the group. There is a well established learning support programme in another college where language support staff visit classes throughout the year to provide information on the different options, encourage learners to progress and provide support and guidance where required. Women from these groups have clear ideas about their future and frequently aspire to graduate professions, and know what they need to do to get there:

> *'You know where you are going next' (Nehal).*

We also encountered women who had suffered from an absence of information or bad advice, like the women who never accessed learning again after their home tuition stopped with no help to find an alternative.

Alia from Somalia said she didn't know whether to start with English or another subject when she arrived from Somalia. She started Information Technology then had to stop because her English wasn't good enough and was on an ESOL waiting list for a long time. After finally entering a class and developing her English she started a childcare course but again had to drop out because she couldn't cope with the writing demands of the course:

> *'If I got advice the first time I started English then I would be at university now, Ten years have been lost for me.' (Alia).*

Zarina's experience below also demonstrates how someone who is keen and committed to education but repeatedly receives inappropriate advice and guidance can miss opportunities.

Zarina's story

Zarina came to the UK from Pakistan 17 years ago as a new bride. She had a degree in political science, history, journalism and advanced Urdu and immediately started learning. She is now fluent in English but despite taking vocational courses including bilingual community care, NVQ teaching assistant, textiles and adult education teacher training, she has been unable to find work commensurate with her abilities.

Zarina feels cheated; that she has consistently been given bad advice and told that courses would lead to jobs only to find out at the end that she needed to attend a different course. As a result, she has moved in and out of factory work, sometimes studying as well as working. She has trained as an adult teacher but failed to secure work and as a result has lowered her horizons and started looking for factory sewing work again. She is very disheartened as she has invested a lot in vocational education and feels it has been a waste of time. Even so she is persisting with learning as it is important to her and keeps her going in the face of her disappointments.

Impact of the learning

Self and family

The overwhelming impact of learning for Bangladeshi, Pakistani, and Somali women is that of increasing confidence and independence. Independence was a life changing outcome for women learning English. They had more choices and could live their lives without relying on others. The learning women said that becoming fluent in English had changed them and made them more confident. They feel independent and able to go out by themselves and can articulate their opinions confidently. They have no problems communicating so they can go about their daily lives better:

> *'Before I didn't go out alone. Now I feel comfortable. I can go anywhere.'*

Teachers also noted that women were more confident in a number of situations, for example, using English, helping their children with their homework, progressing on to other learning, developing new friendships, in social contexts and in their dealings with institutions. Learning has given the women space and time to be themselves and can be a positive, powerful experience as this quote aptly demonstrates:

"Women are glad to have a break from the family and devote some time to themselves for learning. They become women in their own right, not just wives and mothers" (ESOL teacher).

Having confidence means women can realise their personal goals such as learning to drive. Related to a growth in confidence were raised aspirations such as getting a job, studying or volunteering and freedom as they could speak English in new situations. The adjectives used by learning providers here are important to describe the impact learning has on the women; 'confidence', 'aspiration', 'empowerment', 'achievement', 'motivation', 'interaction' and 'integration'.

One provider described some of the changes learning can bring about in the women. In general, learners are really positive about their experiences and about broadening their horizons, for example, understanding more about the different communities in their locality, schools and other faiths. Lots of women spend time in their own communities, never really going outside but learning opens their eyes, boosts their confidence and gives them a sense of self and of their role in society.

The impact of learning for women can be quite remarkable in terms of the changes it brings in their family life; women are able to help their children with their homework and understand the school system. Learners and teachers mentioned being able to communicate with school staff at parents' evenings, for example. One teacher noted that students have moved into family learning activities and are more confident to take part in social activities with their children such as family outings to the funfair.

Most of the women want to continue with learning and some progress on to other courses, others into employment. For example, confidence to progress to GCSE and Level 3 childcare or learning how to drive. Younger women on the whole are optimistic about what education can do for them. They feel they can be the generation that get jobs and can succeed. Overwhelmingly, Somali women see learning as something that benefits the whole community.

"Some of the group have joined other classes to update old skills, or learn new ones. Some have achieved goals, passing the driving theory test, getting a job, or British Citizenship" (ESOL Co-ordinator).

Hali's story

Hali didn't communicate at all in English before she started learning in a one to one context with a volunteer. She was supported by the project's bilingual worker to move into a refuge, as she was the victim of domestic abuse and is now in a safe situation. She has progressed onto an Employability programme because she wanted more intensive learning and has been attending classes regularly. Hali has developed networks and friendships with other learners at the centre and feels supported. She has moved up a level in terms of her speaking and listening.

Learning and employment

Taking part in learning can whet the appetite of Bangladeshi, Pakistani and Somali women for more learning and raise aspirations and hopes to engage in more learning. Many want to move on to vocational training for work. We have seen that some of the younger women are on a track to higher level learning and graduate occupations. Other women tend to view learning for work as a long haul because of their English skills:

'Maybe I'll work in the future. Now my children have grown up I'm quite bored at home but my English is too poor.' (Aspia).

"Students believe that this is something which could be 'for them', not 'for other people'" (ESOL teacher).

Many have high aspirations; for example, one woman is working towards studying to be an optician, one as a nurse and another as a nursery nurse. Rushnara loves children and wants to work with them and is considering childcare, youth work or teaching.

Younger students are more engaged with work aspirations or going to university" (ESOL teacher).

Others, like Amena, want to start as a teaching assistant then work up to a higher-level job while some women have set their sights lower, aiming for factory or cleaning work which they feel doesn't require much English.

It is common for women to progress or plan to progress into vocational learning to support a future job or career. There was an emphasis on courses such as NVQ Childcare or classroom assistant. Many women undertake IT for Small Businesses to support the family business.

The ways in which the women move from learning into employment was less obvious to learning providers as this data isn't routinely collected. One had evidence that women had gone on to find employment in factories, shops and care homes whilst others noted through ad hoc information that women are establishing their own health and beauty businesses. It was observed that it was quite unusual for Somali women to go into work although one provider mentioned that one of her Somali learners had obtained a voluntary post in a local school. Volunteering and aspirations to enter Higher Education were suggested as more probable outcomes.

Shahida's story

Shahida was referred from the Jobcentre to the employability programme. She had no previous formal education. She had a large family and was expected to be the main carer. Consequently, her family didn't prioritise learning for her.

Shahida felt that the rules of the intensive programme meant that her family had to recognise the amount of learning required and prioritise it, which they wouldn't have done otherwise. She felt the amount of learning offered to her was a great opportunity and was a way of getting external recognition for learning. Although she struggled to find the time to commit to learning, she did make some progress. Significantly, after the programme she did voluntary work at a community crèche because she eventually wanted to work in childcare. The initial employability programme helped her focus on what she wanted for herself and take a step towards securing it.

Community

Learning has a number of benefits for the women's engagement with the wider community. They reflected that they are more mobile, independent and more confident to communicate with English speakers. Teachers mentioned spin offs such as volunteering, attending community festivals and events, joining associations such as the Parent Teacher Association or taking part in ESOL networks, interacting with neighbours and the subsequent reduction in isolation. Some of the women had been on class trips to locations such as the library or museum and told tutors that they revisited these places with their families following these visits.

Learners said that attending classes has not necessarily led to greater involvement in community activity with others outside their ethnic and language groups. Some women commented that they don't know what is on offer in their area. College and adult learning students don't access information about community groups through their learning institution. Classes held in community centres gave some women access to information about other activities so that learners in voluntary sector provision were more likely to access opportunities organised by that group, but not necessarily in the community outside. Neither learners nor providers offered examples of learning initiatives specifically designed to foster greater community integration, for instance community capacity building initiatives with language support.

Summary

This section focused on the factors that have enabled Pakistani, Bangladeshi and Somali women to access learning, achieve and progress. A number of common themes emerged. College provision is usually harder to access and usually viewed as for people who already have some education. Community based provision is most accessible for those with little past experience of education and who experience barriers to travelling to college. Alternatives such as home tuition are needed for women not able to access learning outside their homes.

The most effective means of recruiting are word of mouth through friends and family and community based outreach workers. Social events and tasters can be used to attract women and a friendly welcome, enjoyable experience and bilingual staff help to draw them in. Practical support, especially affordable childcare, classes at times to fit with family commitments, an financial assistance where needed supports entry to learning and women only provision opens access to women prevented from entering mixed situations.

The women's motivation and achievement depends on accessible teaching with responsive content that reflects their needs and interests, supportive, approachable teachers, confidence building and recognition of progress through accreditation and other means. Role models, buddying and creating opportunities to speak outside also support progress. Family demands inevitably mean that some women cannot attend as regularly as is desirable. Flexibility to accommodate this erratic attendance means women are not forced to leave and lose their opportunity to learn. High qualify and appropriate information advice and guidance is crucial. The approach to this can raise aspirations whereas advice based on stereotypes or can limit or close down options and opportunities.

Successful learning makes a significant difference to the women's' lives. The benefits include greater independence, increased confidence, higher aspirations, enhanced family life, and employment opportunities Learning did not appear to increase activism in the wider community for the women we talked to, possibly because the content did not reflect this. It di, however, increase their confidence to go out and about, interactions with neighbours and access to community amenities and events.

6. Key themes, conclusions and recommendations

This research set out to investigate the learning journeys of Bangladeshi, Pakistani and Somali women with a particular emphasis on hindrances to participation in learning and the factors that enable the most disadvantaged women within these groups to learn. The stories of the women we encountered contain stark illustrations of the ways in which opportunities for learning can be restricted: by life chances, poverty, living circumstances, the burden of domestic labour and gender oppression from husbands or families. They also shine a light on their strength and resilience and the ways in which some women are supported and others break through barriers to access learning. In turn this has set them on the way to realising their ambitions and dreams. They gave us rich insights into their views on access to learning and what enables them to stay on their learning journeys once they have embarked on them. Dedicated ESOL staff also told us what they did to reach these women and help them stay the course. Together, these discourses give us a deeply textured picture of the intersections of women's lives and learning. This section draws out the implications of the significant themes from the findings for the provision of learning for Bangladeshi, Pakistani and Somali women.

The findings provide an emphatic illustration of the differential experiences and factors affecting participation in learning of women in these groups. The conclusion to be drawn from this is that different approaches are required to ensure that all, especially the most oppressed and excluded, are reached. In this section we suggest a framework to support developments in this direction, and suggest that this framework might also have relevance and application for other groups of learners. Finally, we make recommendations to improve access to learning for these groups of women and for further areas for research.

Not all the same

The statistics show that as a whole, Bangladeshi, Pakistani and Somali women are the groups of adults most excluded from learning in Britain. In general, these women have the lowest levels of qualifications and are the least likely to be taking part in formal learning of any kind. They also have the lowest levels of English language. Some women from these groups have progressed in education and gained degrees, but are less likely to do so than women from other ethnic groups.

The research illustrates the extremely heterogeneous nature of the women. There is diversity within the ethnic groups as well as common experiences that cut across them, and the evidence illuminates some of the vast differences in their circumstances. Factors such as educational backgrounds, marital status, age, life stage and personal and family attitudes all have the potential to make a difference to access to and chances of succeeding in learning. A marked example is the difference between the life situations of young Pakistani and Bangladeshi women in their late teens or early twenties. Those who grew up in the UK often have more freedom and autonomy than women of the same age who came from the sub-continent to marry men raised in the UK.

Hindrances to learning

The findings illustrate different types of barriers to learning faced by the women we studied. These broadly accord with *Cross'* model (1981) that categorises barriers to student engagement as *situational, dispositional and institutional, and the factors* McGivney (2001) identifies as limiting access to learning; personal, cultural, practical, psychological and institutional.

- **personal and cultural** – the women's own, husband and family, community attitudes and expectations of women's place and role

- **practical** – gender oppression – restrictions and violence from families, especially husbands, poor health, old age, caring responsibilities, lack of time

- **psychological** – lack of confidence, feeling too old or too sick to learn

- **Institutional** – lack of information and advice, classes not at the right level, located in inaccessible locations at unsuitable times, fees, lack of affordable childcare.

These findings explain why the women we studied are excluded. We know that many women face the same barriers, especially those related to childcare responsibilities and the findings do not fully answer the question posed earlier- Why are the rates of participation in learning for Pakistani, Bangladeshi and Somali women significantly and consistently lower than those of other groups if they face similar barriers? The answer might lie in the nature, intensity and interactions of these factors in the lives of Pakistani, Bangladeshi and Somali women.

They are more likely to get married than women from other groups and marriage is associated with lower participation. They are more likely to have larger families and more likely to care for their children themselves than use nurseries or child minders which means their opportunities to access learning are restricted for longer periods of their life.

Confidence is frequently cited as a barrier to learning for women from all groups. It becomes a major deterrent when combined with other factors, in particular lack of English. Our study shows the ways in which this limits autonomy and freedom to go out independently which in turn hinders ability to travel to classes. Low levels of English also restrict opportunities to access other vocational, personal or community learning. Different permutations of the above factors combined with the additional layers of language barriers, cultural expectations and in some cases opposition to learning could account for the lower overall participation rates of Bangladeshi, Pakistani and Somali women. A comparative study could provide further explanations.

Attitudinal factors

The findings indicate that attitudinal factors are a powerful determinant of the women's learning. As well as their own beliefs, the attitudes of their own and their husbands' families, their husbands and their children influence priorities and access. As might be expected, these attitudes are diverse and differ within communities.

The findings demonstrate that the primary attitudes influencing access to learning relate to expectations of women's role. In laws often wield large amounts of power over their daughters in law, especially when they live together. This is more common in some of the Pakistani and Bangladeshi families. Women in this position often occupy a low place in the hierarchies of their new families, and this can restrict their opportunities to access learning. In the most extreme cases they are forbidden any access to learning by autocratic husbands who resist them gaining any autonomy or independence. The Somali women in the study generally live apart from their husbands' families. They are more likely to depict themselves as strong-minded women who often deal with their family's affairs and stand up to the men when they disagree with them.

The majority of women we interviewed are married or expect to get married. This has a bearing on their own views and aspirations as well as the attitudes of others. For most, marriage and becoming a mother is an important goal, although younger women are more likely to study further or work between leaving school and marriage. Some families hold rigid views that a married women's sole role is related to household duties: domestic labour and caring for husband, children, other family members and the home. The women in these family circumstances are marginalised, struggle to gain any degree of power and autonomy over their lives and are not allowed to access organised learning.

Other women stressed that over time, attitudes have started to shift and have become more liberal with fewer restrictions placed on their lives. Domestic duties are still regarded as the primary responsibility of women but they are allowed to learn if these duties do not 'suffer.' Yet others are more egalitarian, believing that women and men should have equal rights to learn and work and should share domestic responsibilities and childcare. In general, this is more prevalent amongst younger women who grew up in Britain.

Practical considerations

The norm is for married women to have children and some have large families with more than five children. The women, like all mothers, face the choice of whether to stay home with their children or to leave them to go out to study or work. Situations vary. Many of the women make positive choices not to leave their babies and young children in the care of others. They want to spend this period with their children and believe this will give them the best start in life. Others would like to learn English but cannot find the time, especially if they have large families.

Some women desire to learn English but are prevented by lack of childcare. We learned that some do not want to entrust their children to strangers in nurseries or crèches. Consequently they have to rely on family and are stuck if family are unable or unwilling to assist. Even where women are willing to use crèches or nurseries we heard that many are unable to find affordable childcare to enable them to study.

In addition to childcare, other caring responsibilities especially caring for elders or sick family members takes precedence for some women we interviewed. Provision far from home is a barrier for women who are not able to travel independently, as is lack of confidence, or the need to juggle classes with other responsibilities such as collecting children from school. Potential costs deter some women and lack of information means that others never discover where to find a class.

Life stages

A significant finding emerging from the research is that life stage and age are powerful determinants of women's access to learning. Unmarried young women tend to have more freedom to study or work. The dominant trend is to stop either on marriage or when they have their first baby. Some never return to learning whilst others next think about learning English when their children start school or even wait until they leave home. By then they have lost time. This reinforces their disadvantage and women who took this decision now find learning harder. Looking back, they often regret not having completed their studies and 'wasting' an opportunity for themselves.

Older women not in learning described themselves as too old to learn; they have missed their time to learn, feel they have no need, are no longer capable, or it is not appropriate for older women to learn. In contrast some older women who are learning are very positive about it although they regret waiting. Poor health is another factor preventing access to learning. This was often related to age although not exclusively so.

Ways of reaching out

Evidence from women learners, learning organisers and teachers offered a powerful testimony to the importance and effectiveness of community outreach approaches to enable women from our groups to access learning. Many of the strategies adopted are not new but have been developed and practised since the 1970s. However, in many places they have been neglected as demand for ESOL from more assertive learners has filled classes (Ward 2007). McGivney (2001) notes that the concept of outreach work is rediscovered by different generations of education policy makers and practitioners on a regular basis and stresses the need to reflect on established practice to inform their developments. The community outreach work described by respondents in this study provides one source for this reflection.

Word of mouth emerged as the overarching strategy to reach out to the women and attract them into learning. The ways in which learning institutions deploy word of mouth approaches is also important, and different tactics are appropriate for women in different situations. Failure to recognise and respond to this can mean that the most marginalised women remain outside organised learning provision.

Our research indicated that bilingual community outreach workers who know their area are highly effective at not only spreading the word but also encouraging and supporting women to try learning. They do this by making contact, offering encouragement and building trust. Specific and effective approaches put forward by the most excluded learners included home visits, befriending schemes, interventions to convince families of the benefits of learning and home tuition. These are rarely offered but suggest approaches for developing schemes to reach those least likely to access centre based classes.

Offering appropriate provision in easily accessible spaces regarded as safe or trustworthy by the community is important to attract women unable to travel far. These include learning centres as well as community centres. Respondents emphasised the importance of building trust through long establishment in a community and continuity of provision and staff. The value of offering creative social activities and interesting and enjoyable taster sessions and events to attract and enthuse women was stressed. These activities can reach interested women but the provision on offer must then be offered on terms which enable them to take it up. Childcare is essential. Location, cost, women only spaces, flexibility, interesting, relevant content and teachers with awareness, understanding and experience of working in communities are important ingredients.

Addressing the challenges of supporting women not only to attend but to achieve is critical. Learners articulated this in relation to a combination of what they consistently referred to as 'good teaching' and a range of support measures. For the learners, this 'good teaching' means a teacher they can understand and who understands them, interesting and challenging learning content. For many of our respondents this means addressing the full range of topics relevant to their life including British society, political themes, global issues and religion. Praise and recognition of achievement are also important. For some, exams are important whereas others respond to a range of less formal approaches.

Teachers cited established quality measures such as initial and formative assessment, tutorials, and Individual Learning Plans. Interestingly, none of the women mentioned any of these when asked what helps them stay the course. This echoes the findings of Baynham *et al.* (2007) where only one learner referred to an Individual Learning Plan. This is not to say that these measures do not support learners but they did not articulate their needs in this way. Learning support includes tutorial and classroom support and affordable childcare.

Perhaps one of the strongest messages emerging in relation to practice are that for many of these women, structured learning must be complemented by strong learner-teacher relationships, support from other learners, buddying schemes, role models and social activity which glues them into learning and inspires and enables them to progress. Social activities are used by teachers to broaden knowledge and provide opportunities for using and practising English. The women of all ages find in them a valuable means of fostering friendships and supportive relationships. They encourage each other to learn and for those who are facing home or community disapproval, they break down isolation and engender a sense of solidarity and support that helps them to continue.

Progression to further learning or work aspirations

Once in learning women usually become motivated to continue. Not all women aspire to work but those who do view learning as a passport into interesting careers. The research showed that although women have their own dreams for their futures, providers could be influential. Aspirations varied and women frequently appear to set their sights low. They choose gendered occupations such as cleaning, factory machining, working with children, heath and social care and beauty and often aim for the least skilled lower jobs. Reasons for this include acceptability, and the constraints of English. However, this also raises a number of questions about whether enough is being done to ensure that appropriate approaches to information, advice and guidance are employed to support women to progress. We should ask whether expectations of these groups of women are high enough, whether enough is known about the women's long term goals and whether enough is being done to ensure that women from these groups are able to reach their potential in the UK.

While lower paid or lower status employment might be realistic options for some women, the horizons of others appear to be limited in part by the lack of advice, information and progression pathways to higher-level occupations. It was noticeable that women who attend provision that offers vocational information and advice and bridges to progress often aim higher than others. The importance of role models was a recurring theme yet few providers offer role model schemes, perhaps because of resource constraints or lack of confidence or knowledge to establish these schemes.

Community participation

As discussed in the context section, the concept of community cohesion is far from straightforward. The research revealed interesting perspectives on the notion of community which most of the women interviewed define in relation to their ethnic group and not their geographical area. In general the two were co-terminus, but even women who live in ethnically mixed or primarily white area areas referred to their community in terms of their ethnic group.

The majority of women interviewed choose to live in areas where there are high numbers of people from their ethnic group. This is usually a positive choice made for reasons that will be familiar to most readers; the desire to live near friends and family with amenities in easy reach and to feel safe. There are extremely high levels of community cohesion within these communities as family, friends and neighbours form strong social and support networks. Even the women who are oppressed at home find solidarity and support from other women in their community. Where the women avoid their English neighbours it is usually for reasons of safety as they experience real or actual threats of crime and harassment and some are subjected to racism.

At the same time, lack of English does inhibit some women from communicating with their English-speaking neighbours. There are relatively high levels of involvement in communal leisure activities, informal support networks, or voluntary organisations within their own communities. In contrast there is a noticeable lack of activity outside, and only a small minority of women volunteer or intend to volunteer in the future. The women not in organised learning tend not to take up opportunities such as Sure Start, use amenities such as libraries and parks or join community groups or take up voluntary work in mixed ethnic group. Women engaged in learning reported more use of amenities but, in general, not greater involvement in volunteering. English is one of a number of reasons, but lack of interest or inclination, lack of time or opportunity or no information or encouragement from community organisations were also cited. This suggests that English language skills might be a condition for involvement, but by themselves will not automatically bring about greater community cohesion and engagement.

The conversations demonstrate that it is difficult to impose community cohesion as you can't force people to mix with each other if they do not want to. Cohesion needs to grow from the ground. Learning can provide some of the conditions for this, but only if others are in place, especially safety, interventions to promote active encouragement, mutual commitment and respect. However, we found little evidence of learning that had the specific aim of fostering cohesion either in discrete groups or in mixed community based groups and more models for this are urgently needed.

Learning does not take place in a vacuum and must relate to the contexts of place as well as of individual lives. Approaches offered without taking these factors into account can offer ineffective solutions. Providers will need to look at their advances and approaches in the context they move into. It is imperative that providers avoid the danger of treating neighbourhoods where these women live as empty vessels waiting to fill with classes, or indeed to treat the women themselves as empty vessels to be filled with learning. As we found, there are dynamic networks operating in many communities and these have enormous potential to support efforts to reach women.

Planning and Outreach Framework

The differences in women's attitudes and circumstances sketched out above means that access to learning plays out in very different ways for different women and at different stages in their lives. Recognition of this can support the development of more nuanced strategies to identify which groups are represented in learning and who is missing. Four clear groups have emerged illustrated in the framework diagram below. Differentiated approaches can be deployed to respond to their different situations to bring about greater inclusion of all, including the most marginalised and excluded women.

We have developed a framework that can be used to support the identification of need in an area and the development of focused engagement strategies to formulate an inclusive response. This framework identifies four different types of women who have different learning aspirations and/or face different barriers to learning. The inner squares indicate strategies for attracting and supporting these different groups into learning. The lines between the groups are dotted to illustrate that the boundaries between the groups are porous. In other words some women may have attributes from adjacent groups and others move between the groups at different stages. Similarly outreach strategies are not necessarily restricted to any one type and different approaches might be effective at different stages.

Planning and outreach framework

Learning positive	Learning optimistic
Positive attitudes + few/no practical barriers	Positive attitudes + some practical and/or physical barriers

	Outreach workers/learning ambassadors *Childcare/crèche provision* *Local classes* *Flexible provision* *Allow to leave and return* *Support during maternity leave* *Flexible timing* *Women only provision* *Taster activities* *Relevant content* *Appropriate IAG* *Appropriate progression routes*	*Childcare commitments* *Caring responsibilities* *Lack of time* *Distance to provision*
Appropriate signposting *Appropriate IAG* *Interesting provision* *Progression routes*		
Childcare commitments (might plan to learn at a later stage) *Caring responsibilities* *Poor health* *Age*	*Promotion using role models* *Persuaders* *Social activities* *Home tuition/street groups* + *leanring optimistic strategies*	*Befrienders* *Family mediators* *Home tuition* + *learning optimistic strategies*	*Gender oppression* *Domestic violence*

Negative attitudes + some physical and practical Barriers	Positive attitudes + severe gender oppression, practical and physical barriers
Learning Negative	Learning pessimistic

● **Learning positive** women are highly motivated to learn and face minimal serious restrictions or hindrances to learning. For these women the challenge is one of supply; to direct resources to offer enough learning to satisfy this appetite. However, this alone will be insufficient. Those offering learning will need to ensure they do everything possible to enable women to stay with it, to make progress in learning, to raise their aspirations and set them on the path to achieving these aspirations.

● **Learning optimistic** women would like to learn but face practical and/or physical obstacles such as lack of good quality affordable childcare, accessible, relevant provision, or lack of time. Their options are limited by practical barriers that must be considered when planning learning and recruiting women. Bridges to help make entry not only possible but easy are needed. Once engaged, women will need ongoing support to assist them to stay and progress.

● **Learning negative** women are not currently interested in learning. They face barriers such as domestic or caring responsibilities or very poor health. Some can manage or get by and are not motivated to progress further. Others have made a decision not to learn at this stage but might be persuaded now or in the future. Others are resistant for health reasons or because they consider themselves too old to learn.

● **Learning pessimistic** women would like to learn but are unable to access learning outside the home because they are fettered by gender oppression, domestic burdens or ill health.

They are unlikely to be able to access learning outside the home as they live in circumstances in which they have few choices or are denied opportunities for autonomous decision-making.

Only the learning negative group is resistant to learning. Women in the other groups would like to learn but face different hindrances. Recognising the differences in women's freedom to choose, and the different nature of the constraints on their choices highlights the complexity of this divergence. It follows, therefore, that different strategies and solutions are needed to reach different women. The signposting that can get some to class will go nowhere to touch the lives of women tied to the home. Reaching those who are most isolated and oppressed poses greater challenges. There appear to be smaller numbers of women in these groups, but if strategies are not devised to reach them they are likely to remain hidden from learning.

Strategies to reach women

Learning positive women do not encounter major difficulties accessing classes. The priority for work with them is to support them to stay their course and ensure that appropriate advice and guidance is offered throughout their learning journeys to support them to raise their aspirations and make realistic decisions about their future that enables them to achieve their dreams wherever possible.

Learning optimistic women want to learn but face barriers to learning. Strategies to enable them to access learning will focus on learning that removes as many of these obstacles as possible. These obstacles can be predicted in general but work to gather information about the particulars in different neighbourhoods will enable focused interventions that can make more of a difference.

Learning negative women are the most challenging group. It has to be acknowledged that some are highly unlikely to enter learning. Appropriate and sensitive interventions might move other women from this group into another category. Mothers staying at home with young children would be one priority for this work. The learning negative mothers we interviewed believe staying home gives their young children the best start. Approaches that convince them and their families of the benefits to children's health and education of mothers who speak English could go a long way to persuading them to participate in learning sooner rather than later. Tied to accessible provision and acceptable and affordable models of childcare support, this could offer a powerful approach to widening the participation of these mothers.

Learning pessimistic women want to learn but face severe practical, physical and attitudinal barriers. The most oppressed women are in this group, including those not allowed to leave the home to learn. It is important, therefore, that initiatives to reach them are put in place. For some, the only option might be to provide starting points through home tuition offered to individuals or small groups of women. Sensitive approaches to persuade families of the benefits of learning might accompany these activities to enable women in this group to progress in the future. Identifying appropriate people to undertake this work will be needed, with awareness of the pitfalls. A particular challenge will be identifying individuals acceptable to the family but who do not hold attitudes that reinforce and perpetuate the women's oppressive situations.

The advantages of using this framework to underpin a differentiated approach are that it provides a tool to support those tasked with planning and providing learning to analyse which groups are already in learning and which are missing. The framework can then be used to support the development of recruitment and support strategies to reach the different groups. This also makes economic sense. Appropriate, targeted action is likely to be more effective but will incur additional costs. Outreach work, for instance, needs to be organised and staffed and additional budget allocations will be required to support this work. Adopting a differentiated approach can ensure that activity can be directed to benefit learners and potential learners in the most cost effective manner.

It is vital to recognise that where women experience disadvantage or racism, learning works best as an aspect of multi-dimensional approaches that address a range of the factors associated with injustice and discrimination. There must be an awareness of why things change and what appropriate interventions are. Working in partnership with other agencies and organisations is key. The voluntary and community sector also has an important part to play, not least in its ability to reach and to understand the circumstances of these women. However, they, like other providers, will need to critically examine their approaches and practice to ensure they are appropriate for different groups of women. Teachers, outreach workers and champions must be equipped with the skills and understanding to work in this manner and with each other as well as the myriad individuals, front line workers and agencies that also have a stake in these neighbourhoods. These approaches might demand new ways of thinking and working, and they can be challenging. However, they must be tackled in pursuit of a more equal and just society in which the most excluded Bangladeshi, Pakistani and Somali women are enabled to move from the margins and gain more independence, equality and choice.

7. Recommendations

A differentiated approach

We recommend that a differentiated model be adopted to identify the needs of women in different communities and put in place appropriate targeted strategies to reach these women and plan learning to meet their needs.

The framework on page 72 can be used as a model to identify differentiated approaches and strategies to reach different women, including the most marginalised. These are set out below. We stress again that the lines between the groups are porous which means in this context that some strategies can be appropriate for women in one or more groups. As the barriers to learning are common in the wider population, this framework might have wider application with other groups, although the particulars and strategies to reach different groups of adults might differ.

Cross-departmental and interagency working to connect the inclusion of Pakistani Bangladeshi and Somali women in learning provision to other services and community initiatives is crucial. One way of thinking about building this is partnership working to link in to community wellbeing, community cohesion and health agendas. Connecting to health services is also important as health workers are an excellent conduit for reaching women outside the learning territory. As learning enhances wellbeing, improves health and reduces stress (Schuller *et al.* 2004) this will ensure that women reap the wider benefits of learning and help these other agencies achieve their aims.

Actions

In order to support this model the following should be put into place

The government should:

- support the development of a national programme to explore effective forms of community outreach strategies to reach the most excluded women

- fund action research to explore and develop approaches to offering role model and mentoring schemes to disseminate to all providers

- establish and fund a national programme to develop and test approaches to support women to:

  - access services

  - have a voice in service development and delivery

  - enhance their capacity to work with others to act for improvements in their neighbourhoods

Local planning and funding agencies and partnerships should:

- adopt a differentiated model for identifying need and reaching all learners, especially the most excluded in the areas in which they work

- identify and explore opportunities for, and approaches to, cross agency working

- recognise and draw on the potential of the voluntary and community sector to reach these women and identify resources to support them to do so

- allocate resources for outreach work and community engagement activities

- plan provision to meet all needs in an area including Entry levels 1 and 2 and literacy for those at these levels

- offer appropriate training to the statutory and voluntary sector workforces and volunteers working with these women. This will include awareness raising, confidence in using approaches that liberate and empower women, and, for teachers, develop understanding of the contexts in which they are working, the most effective approaches to offer and skills in teaching learners with few or no literacy skills.

- develop funded buddying, role model, and mentoring schemes that operate across local areas.

Providers should:

- adopt a differentiated approach to identifying barriers to learning faced by women in the communities they serve

- ensure that learning offers are rooted in communities and different strategies are in place to reach different groups

- ensure that learning offered is relevant to women and their communities as well as rigorous and high quality

- ensure that learners have a voice in what is offered and how it is promoted

- develop home tuition schemes to take learning to women who cannot access it outside their homes

- put in place role model and mentoring schemes where women, who have achieved, including language learners, use their experience to inspire and support others to follow

- put in place effective information, advice and guidance strategies to support learners to aim for heightened but realistic aspirations, and progression pathways to support their achievement.

Areas for further research

This research interviewed a range of women in our quest to understand their attitudes to learning and the factors that make learning difficult and unlock doors to enable women to both access learning and persist. Our sample included women who grew up in the UK and are fluent in English. Their perspectives were valuable to the research in that they demonstrated both how attitudes are changing and shone some light on how women from these groups who have benefited from education and are fluent in English fare as adult women. However, it was beyond the scope of this study to investigate the access of this group to wider learning provision in any detail. This could, however, prove a fruitful area for further research.

We focused on Pakistani, Bangladeshi and Somali women as they are amongst the most disadvantaged groups in the UK in terms of poverty and access to learning and employment. Of course there are exceptions to this and there were women from these groups who were less disadvantaged. Similarly, in the course of our research we encountered women from other minority ethnic groups who were deeply disadvantaged in terms of poverty and access. Further research could identify similarities and differences in their patterns of exclusion and strategies that enable greater access and success. This could test the applicability of our framework to other groups. Equally, we would advise planners and providers to establish who is excluded in their area and direct provision and strategies to them.

In the course of our research we found very little literature on the lives, aspirations and learning needs of Somali women. This research starts to scratch the surface but more knowledge would help develop responses that secure more equity for this group of women.

Areas for further research are

- comparative studies to shine more light on the reasons for the persistence of higher levels of exclusion amongst Pakistan, Bangladeshi and Somali women

- investigate Somali women's lives, aspirations and in order to offer learning to bring about greater inclusion and equity, approaches which include them

- how to meet the language learning needs of young women, especially unaccompanied asylum seekers

- the barriers and enablers to learning for Pakistani, Bangladeshi and Somali women educated in the UK

- the similarities and differences in patterns of women's exclusion from learning and strategies that enable greater access and success

- research effective strategies to attract mothers of babies and toddlers into learning through the agency of community champions and health and early years workers.

- the role of language in fostering community cohesion

- research the application of the differentiated model to other groups of potential learners.

References

Aldridge, F. and Tuckett, A. (2003), *Light and Shade. A NIACE briefing on participation in adult learning by minority ethnic adults*, Leicester: NIACE.

Aldridge, F., Dutton, Y. and Tuckett, A. (2006), *In the spotlight. A NIACE briefing on participation in learning by adults from minority ethnic groups*, Leicester: NIACE.

Aldridge, F., Lamb, H. and Tuckett, A. (2008), *Are we closing the gap A NIACE briefing on participation in learning by adults from minority ethnic groups*, Leicester: NIACE

Aston, J., Hooker, H., Page, R. and Wilson, R. (2007), *Pakistani and Bangladeshi women's attitudes to work and family. Research Report No 458*, London: Department for Work and Pensions.

Atubo, M. R. and Batterbury, S. (2001), *Coping with environmental change: the experience of Somali refugee women in a West London housing estate*, London: London School of Economics and Political Science, http://www.lse.ac.uk/collections/DESTIN/pdf/WP11.pdf (accessed 4 June 2008).

Baynham, M., Roberts, C., Cooke, M., Simpson, J., Ananiadou, K., Callaghan, J., McGoldrick, J. and Wallace, C. (2007), *Effective teaching and learning: ESOL,* London: NRDC.

BEAP Community Partnership (2004), *Bangladeshi Women's Research*, http://www.beapuk.org/Documents/Bangladeshi%20Women's%20Research.DOC (accessed 4 June 2008).

Bloch, A. and Atfield, G. (2002), *The Professional Capacity of Somali Nationals In England*, Goldsmiths College, University of London, http://fmo.qeh.ox.ac.uk/Repository/getPdf.asp?Path=Oxford1/1604/05/02&PageNo=1 (accessed 4 June 2008).

Botcherby, S. (2006), *Pakistani, Bangladeshi and Black Caribbean women and employment survey: aspirations, experiences and choices*, Manchester: Equal Opportunities Commission.

Carneiro, P., Meghir, C. and Parey, M. (2006), *Intergenerational effects of mother's schooling on children's outcomes: causal links and transmission channels,* London: UCL.

Cole, I. and Robinson, D (2003), *Somali housing experiences in England*, Sheffield: Sheffield Hallam University.

Commission on Integration and Cohesion (2007), *Our Shared Future,* http://www.integrationandcohesion.org.uk/~/media/assets/www.integrationandcohesion.org.uk/our_shared_futu re%20pdf.ashx (accessed 4 June 2008)

Craig, G., Adamson, S., Ali, N., Ali, S., Atkins, L., Dadze-Arthur, A., Elliott, C., McNamee, S. and Murtuja, B. (2007), *National evaluation report. Sure Start and Black and Minority Ethnic Populations, Research Report NESS/2007/FR/020*, London: DfES, http://www.dfes.gov.uk/research/data/uploadfiles/NESS2007FR020.pdf, (accessed 4 June 2008).

Cross, K. (1981) *Adults as learners*, San Francisco, Jossey-Bass.

Crozier, G., Davies, J., Khatun, S. and Booth, D. (2004), *Parents, Children and the School Experience: Asian Families' Perspectives End of Award Report*, http://my.sunderland.ac.uk/web/projects/apsse/bresearch_report/documents/REPORTREVISED-7-1-05.pdf (accessed 4 June 2008).

Dale, A, Shaheen, N., Kalra, V. and Fieldhouse, E. (2000), *Routes into education and employment for young Pakistani and Bangladeshi women in the UK*. ESRC Future of Work Programme Working Paper No.10, http://www.ccsr.ac.uk/publications/occasion/Occ19.pdf, (accessed 4 June 2008).

Dalziel, D. and Sofres, T.N. (2005), *Qualitative Evaluation of the ESOL Pathfinder Projects,* London: DfES.

DfES (2006), *Ethnicity and Education: The Evidence on Minority Ethnic Pupils aged 5–16*, London: DfES, http://publications.teachernet.gov.uk/eOrderingDownload/DFES-0208-2006.pdf (accessed 4 June 2008).

DfES (2007), *Race Equality impact assessment on proposed changes to the funding arrangements for English for Speakers of Other Languages and asylum seeker eligibility for Learning and Skills Council Further education funding – report and emerging proposals,* London: DfES.

DIUS (2008), *DIUS Consultations: Focusing English for Speakers of Other Languages (ESOL) on Community Cohesion,* http://www.esolconsultation.org.uk/, (accessed 4 June 2008).

Gregory, E. (1996), 'Learning from the Community: A family literacy project with Bangladeshi-origin children in London', in Wolfendale, S. and Topping, K. (eds.), *Family Involvement in Literacy,* London: Cassell.

Hall, K., Bance, J. and Denton, N. (2004), *Diversity and Difference: Minority Ethnic*

Mothers and Childcare, London: Women's Equality Unit.

Harries, B., Richardson, L. and Soteri-Proctor, A. (2008) *Housing Aspirations for a new generation. Perspectives from white and south Asian British women,* http://www.jrf.org.uk/bookshop/eBooks/2236-women-housing-ethnicity.pdf (accessed 8 July 2008)

Home Office (2005a), *Improving Opportunity, Strengthening Society: The government's strategy to increase race equality and community cohesion*, London: Home Office

Home Office (2005b), *Integration matters: A National Strategy for Refugee Integration*, London: Home Office

Hudson, M., Philips, J., Ray, K. and Barnes, H. (2007), *Social cohesion in diverse communities*, York: Joseph Rowntree Foundation.

ICAR (2007), *The Somali Refugee Community in the UK*, London: City University, http://www.icar.org.uk/, (accessed 4 June 2008).

Jarman, E. (2007), *Involving Asian Families in Learning: A toolkit for practitioners*, The Basic Skills Agency at NIACE, Leicester: NIACE.

Joseph Rowntree Foundation (2007), *The role of higher education in providing opportunities for South Asian women*, http://www.jrf.org.uk/knowledge/findings/socialpolicy/2058.asp, (accessed 4 June 2008).

Joseph Rowntree Foundation (2008), *Immigration, faith and cohesion,*
http://www.jrf.org.uk/knowledge/findings/socialpolicy/pdf/2190.pdf, (accessed 4 June 2008).

Kofman, E., Raghuram, P. and Merefield, M. (2005), *Gendered Migrations: Towards gender sensitive policies in the UK,* London: Institute for Public Policy Research.

Kyambi, S. (2005), *Beyond Black and White. Mapping new immigrant communities*, Institute for Public Policy Research.

Law, C. and Weaver, S. (2007), *Black and Minority Ethnic Groups and Skills for Life: Who are the Priority Groups? A Review of the Literature and Data*, Leicester: NIACE.

McGivney, V. (2001) *Fixing or Changing the Pattern?,* Leicester: NIACE

NIACE (2006), '*More than a language...*' Final report of the NIACE Committee of Inquiry on English for Speakers of other Languages (ESOL), Chaired by Derek Grover CB, Leicester: NIACE.

O' Leary, D. (2008) *A common language, Making English work for London,* London: Demos

Office for National Statistics (2007), *Update on the Improving Migration and Population Statistics (IMPS) Project -August 2006,*
http://www.statistics.gov.uk/about/data/methodology/specific/population/future/imps/updates/downloads
/Update_on_the_Improving_Migration_and_Population_Statistics.pdf, (accessed 4 June 2008).

Platt, L. (2007), *Poverty and ethnicity in the UK*, York: Joseph Rowntree Foundation,
http://www.jrf.org.uk/bookshop/eBooks/2006-ethnicity-poverty-UK.pdf, (accessed 4 June 2008).

Rees, S., Savitzky, F. and Malik, A. (eds.) (2003), *On the Road. Journeys in family learning,* London: London Language and Literacy Unit.

Roberts, C., Baynham, M., Shrubshall, P., Barton, D., Chopra, P., Cooke, M., Hodge, R., Pitt, K., Schellekens, P., Wallace, C. and Whitfield, S. (2004), *English for Speakers of Other Languages (ESOL) – case studies of provision, learners' needs and resources,* London: NRD

Robinson, D., Reeve, K and Casey, R. (2007), *The housing pathways of new immigrants*, York: Joseph Rowntree Foundation.

SHM (2007), *Engaging Muslims in Learning. Preliminary report on findings for LSC E&D Committee. May 2007*, London: SHM.

Simpson, L., Phillips, D and Ahmed, S. (2007), *Oldham and Rochdale: race, housing and community cohesion*, Oldham: Oldham and Rochdale Housing Market Renewal Pathfinder,
http://www.ccsr.ac.uk/research/documents/CCSRRacehousingandcommunitycohesionFeb07.pdf, (accessed 4 June 2008).

Schuller, T., Preston, J., Hammond, C., Brassett-Grundy, A. and Bynner, J. (2004), *The Benefits of Learning,* London: RoutledgeFalmer.

Tackey, N.D., Casebourne, J., Aston, J., Ritchie, H., Sinclair, A., Tyers, C., Hurstfield, J., Willison, R. and Page, R. (2006), *Barriers to employment for Pakistanis and Bangladeshis in Britain*. Research Report No.360, London: Department for Work and Pensions, http://www.dwp.gov.uk/asd/asd5/rports2005-2006/rrep360.pdf, (accessed 4 June 2008).

Tyrer, D. and Ahmad, F. (2006), *Muslim Women and Higher Education: Identities, Experiences and Prospects. A Summary Report*, Liverpool John Moores University and European Social Fund, http://image.guardian.co.uk/sys-files/Education/documents/2006/08/02/muslimwomen.pdf, (accessed 4 June 2008).

Ward, J. (2007), *ESOL: The context for the UK today*, Leicester: NIACE.

White, L. and Weaver, S. (2007), *Curriculum for Diversity Guide*, Leicester: NIACE.

Wigfield, A. (2007), *Attitudes to work amongst Pakistani and Bangladeshi women in West Yorkshire*, Sheffield: Policy Evaluation Group.

Wilson, A. (2006), *Dreams, Questions, Struggles. South Asian Women in Britain*, London: Pluto Press.

Yeandle, S., Stiell, B. and Buckner, L. (2006), *Ethnic Minority Women and Access to the Labour Market. Synthesis Report*, Sheffield Hallam University: Centre for Social Inclusion, http://www.shu.ac.uk/research/ceir/downloads/S4BMEWomenSynthesis_281106.pdf, (accessed 4 June 2008).

Zetter, R., Griffiths, D., Sigona, N., Flynn, D., Pasha, T. and Beynon, R. (2006*), Immigration, social cohesion and social capital. What are the links?*, York: Joseph Rowntree Foundation, http://www.jrf.org.uk/bookshop/eBooks/9781899354440.pdf, (accessed 4 June 2008).

Research Framework – Community Researcher Interview Questions

What learning journeys work for Bangladeshi, Pakistani and Somali women?

Research Framework (to support interviews with Pakistani, Bangladeshi and Somali women not currently in learning provision)

Please try to gather as much in-depth information as possible. Ask your interviewees for reasons for their answers 'Why do you say/think that?' and when they say something that might be interesting 'Can you tell more about that please?

1. Personal information

Name (will be kept anonymous)

Pakistani/ Bangladeshi/Somali

Blackburn/Leicester/London

Age

Marital status

Children number and ages

Languages spoken/written

Length of time in UK

Reason for coming to the UK

2. Education

Background

Education in home country (number of years, level, qualifications etc.)

Education in UK (if any) – subject, level, qualifications etc.)

What is the education of others in your family? (immediate family e.g. husband and children) (if any) – subject, level, qualifications etc.)

What do these family members think about women's education? (should they learn, what, how, where etc.)

What do people in your community think about women's education? (should they learn, what, how, where etc.)

3. Learning English

Do you speak English – what level?

Do you write English – what level?

What can you do using English? (prompts e.g. talking to teachers at your child's school, talk to neighbours, work, accessing services)

What are the things that you can't do because of English?

What are the things you would like to do if you had more English?

Have you learnt English in the past?

How did it help you (ask about self confidence, helping children at school/nursery, health work, community)

Why did you stop?

What do your family think about you learning English?

What do other people in your community think about you learning English?

Do you think this has changed? In what ways?

Would you like to learn English? Reasons for your answer

What stops you learning English?

What would help you to learn English?

4. Other learning

What other learning have you done in the past?

Why did you stop?

Would you like to do other learning now?

What stops you?

What would help you?

What do your family think about you learning?

What do other people in your community think about you learning?

5. Work

Tell me about work you have done – in your home country/ the UK?

If you worked – what difference did English make? (to the sort of job you had/ to your relationships with your workmates?)

If you didn't work why was this?

Did other things make a difference to your work?

What do your family think about you/women working? Does this depend on age, children etc.?

What do people in your community think about you/women working? Does this depend on age, children etc.?

6. Community

Tell me about the community you live in.

How do you get on with other people – neighbours, other mothers etc. from the same background/ other groups?

Are you active in your community (go to social groups such as mums and toddlers, school governor, tenants groups etc)

Why do you do this?

Does English make a difference to how much you are involved with your neighbours and the wider community?

What other things make a difference?

If you had the choice would you like to stay where you live or move somewhere different (ask for reasons for the answer)?

If somewhere different what kind of community?

What learning journeys work for Bangladeshi, Pakistani and Somali women?

Please return the completed questionnaire by FRIDAY 28th MARCH 2008.

> Name of organisation
>
> Type of provider
>
> Your name
>
> Your role in the organisation
>
> Contact details:
>
> Address
>
> Telephone number
>
> Email address

Please describe your learning provision that is attended by these women:
Please give a brief description of the learners (backgrounds, ages, English language levels, religion etc.)

Recruitment

> How do you recruit Bangladeshi, Pakistani and/or Somali women?
>
> (e.g. outreach work, community contacts, publicity, taster sessions)
>
> What are the most effective strategies you use?
>
> Please describe in detail your three most effective strategies.
>
> Tell us why they work.
>
> What barriers do the women have to overcome to attend your provision?
>
> How do you support them to do this?

Learning provision

> What strategies do you use to support the women to stay the course?
>
> What works best?
>
> Why are these approaches effective?
>
> What approaches do you have to support them to progress in learning?
>
> Which of these approaches work?

Why are they effective?

Impact of the learning

What difference has the learning made to the women? Please comment on the relevant categories below. Please say how you know and give examples.

Personal

Family life

Life in the wider community (e.g. relationships with neighbours, taking part in activities, events and groups, community activism)

Further learning

Work (paid employment and voluntary work)

We will be following up some providers to explore interesting practice in more detail. Would you be willing to take part in:

a telephone interview?

a project visit?

Thank you very much for taking the time to fill in this questionnaire. If you would like further information about our research please contact:

Jane Ward jane.ward@niace.org.uk or
Rachel Spacey rachel.spacey@niace.org.uk

Appendix 3:

Telephone interview schedule

What learning journeys work for Bangladeshi, Pakistani and Somali women?

Please probe for as much detail as possible about what providers do to support Bangladeshi, Pakistani and Somali women to access and progress in learning, the reasons they are successful and the difference successful learning makes to their lives.

Where students are learning with students from a wider range of backgrounds, please ask providers to answer the questions in relation to Bangladeshi, Pakistani and/or Somali women.

Name of organisation

Type of provider

Your name

Your role in the organisation

Contact details:

Address

Phone

Email

1. Please describe your learning provision that is attended by these women

2. Please give a brief description of the learners (backgrounds, ages, English language levels, religion etc.)

3. Recruitment

3.1 How do you recruit Bangladeshi, Pakistani and/or Somali women?
(e.g. outreach work, community contacts, publicity, taster sessions)

3.2 What are the most effective strategies you use?
Please describe in detail your most effective strategies

3.3 Tell us why they work

3.4 What barriers do the women have to overcome to attend your provision?

3.5 How do you support them to do this?

4. Learning provision

    4.1 What strategies do you use to support the women to stay the course?
        (Refer back to the barriers identified)

    4.2 What works best?

    4.3 Why are these approaches effective?

    4.4 What approaches do you have to support them to make progress in learning?

    4.5 Which of these approaches work?

    4.6 Why are they effective?

5. Impact of the learning

What difference has the learning made to the women? Please comment on the relevant categories below. Please say how you know and give examples.

    5.1 Personal

    5.2 Family life

    5.3 Life in the wider community (e.g. relationships with neighbours, taking part in activities, events and groups, community activism)

    5.4 Further learning

    5.5 Work (paid employment and voluntary work)

Programme visits

Preston College (outreach)

Liverpool Community College

Manchester Adult Education Service

Shama Women's Centre, Leicester

Tower Hamlets College